ISLAMIC STUDIES IN INDIA

About the Author

Dr. Mohamed Taher (b. 1955), is a staff of the American Studies Research Centre, Hyderabad, India. He has worked primarily as a library professional, but has also taught, at times, Library Science students in different institutions.

He has a Ph. D. from Calicut University in the field of Library Science. He has his Master's degree in History, Islamic Studies and Library Science.

He has extensively contributed to various Indian and foreign journals, like *ILA Bulletin, IASLIC Bulletin, Lucknow Librarian, Islamic Culture, Islam and the Modern Age, Muslim Education Quarterly, American Journal of Islamic Social Sciences, Collection Management, International Library Review*, etc. He has reviewed many books, which have been published in *Asian Profile*, *Muslim World Book Review, Indian Book Chronicle*, etc.

He is presently in USA as a fulbright visitor. His other books ready for press are: *Librarianship and Library Science in India: An outline of Historical Perspectives; Muslims in India: A Bibliographical Study*; and, *Quotable quotes in Library and Information Science.*

Concepts in Communication Informatics & Librarianship-22

Gen. Editor: **S.P. Agrawal**

ISLAMIC STUDIES IN INDIA

A Survey of Human, Institutional and Documentary Sources

MOHAMED TAHER

CONCEPT PUBLISHING COMPANY PVT. LTD.
NEW DELHI-110059

ISBN-13: 978-81-7022-359-7

Edition 2017

Published and Printed by

Concept
Since 1974

Concept Publishing Company Pvt. Ltd.
A/15-16, Commercial Block, Mohan Garden
New Delhi-110059 (India)
T: 25351460, 25351794, *F*: 091-11-25357109
E: publishing@conceptpub.com, W: www.conceptpub.com
Editorial Office: H-13, Bali Nagar, New Delhi-110 015, India.

DEDICATED TO
Ibn Ruqia Ali Muhammed Ismail, M.A.
my Father :
who has been
friend, philosopher and guide

GENERAL EDITOR'S INTRODUCTION

WITH THE present publication, CICIL fills a void in handy reference works dealing with a subject universe of great moment.

If Islam hits the headlines off and on, it is because of political turmoil or social upheavals far and near.

However, Islam is very much more than mere passing waves in currents of history. Islamic studies relate to scholastic pursuits of basic fundamental type covering a wide range of subjects.

In India, there is need now, more than ever before, for a dissemination of knowledge about Islam and the contribution it has made to culture, civilization and thought.

And what better way could there be to make an acquaintance with these than to know about the sources and the resources available here.

Dr. M. Taher who is academically and professionally well qualified has listed them together for us in the following pages.

Besides the obvious usefulness to a librarian, an undergrade can turn to it to see which academic institution he could join; a doctoral aspirant can find what topics have been researched into, a scholar can know about other of his ilk to exchange views or elicit opinion, a foreigner can discover something about places to visit in his itinerary or look up some unfamiliar words.

CICIL, outside of E & O, will await suggestions, to have newer editions as a regular feature.

S.P. AGRAWAL

PREFACE

THE REFERENCE books covered in this book represent all recent publications within and outside India (1971–1989).

The journals cover research-oriented titles as well as general purpose ones in leading Indian languages.

Doctoral research work which has been completed in Indian and foreign universities, right from 1900 to date, are covered.

A brief description of prominent cities with strong Muslim cultural connections.

Identification of specialists/writers who are living and available in and outside the Indian universities. Subject specialisation has been incorporated wherever data existed.

Institutions included are both traditional and modern; like *madrasas*, private and public bodies established to promote the study and research and information centres specialising in the area of Islam and Muslims in India.

Glossary incorporates terms common in usage among Muslims — theological, collquial, etc.

Sources consulted for compilation of this *Encyclopaedia Indicus Islamicus* are varied: human, documentary and institutional. The documentary sources are listed in the last pages. Words are insufficient to express thanks to hundreds of individuals, institutions, etc. who provided this material.

The drudgery of this compilation was undertaken by a single individual. No doubt there might be a great deal of material that could not be covered in this work. All errors and omissions are mine. Any suggestions to improve this database are welcomed. Nevertheless, several sources have indirectly helped me do this.

CONTENTS

1. INTRODUCTION

INTRODUCTION

IN RECENT times, Islamic studies has assumed an independent status, which is no longer a part of Oriental Studies. The independence has been evolutionary and today it is another region of "area studies". Islamic studies is by its nature inter- and multi-disciplinary. The main concern of Islamic studies specialists, i.e., the Islamists (or Islamicists) is religion, history, social, cultural, economical, political and scientific. They are not just concerned with Islamic religion, theology, philosophy, but also with the whole civilization including of course, the languages in which this civilization has expressed itself.

Islamic studies is a catch phrase/a cover term, which has come to mean many things for many people. There is hardly any clear-cut, specified or specifiable definition that may be quoted as standard. However, we can explain it by saying that it encompasses to a large extent anything and everything on Islam and Muslims. There are two schools of thought on Islamic studies, one view it as an area of study and the other views it as a discipline. By all possible indications it points out that there is no separation of literature of religious and secular type, or that of matter and spirit, and it specifically deals with any publication by or on Muslims and Islam.

Islam literally means peace and submission. To quote Justice Syed Amir Ali from his *Spirit of Islam* (1922) "Salam (Salama) in its primary sense, means 'to be tranquil', 'at rest', 'to have done one's duty', 'to have paid up', 'to be at perfect peace', etc." In its secondary sense, it means "surrender oneself to Him *(Allah)* with whom peace is made". Muslim literally means, one who submits or surrenders oneself to Him.

History of Islam in India is of one thousand years. Muslims constitute a significant element of Indian Society – i.e., nearly 11 per cent (the biggest minority in the country). The Muslims in India have their origins as traders, saints and *sufis*, and rulers. A good number of them is local converts. Historical documents suggest that the first entrants were Muslim Arabs who landed on the Malabar Coast in the end of the seventy century. Following the Muslim Arabs, Persians, Turks and Afghans started pouring in (See Syed Abdul Lateef, *Outline of the Cultural History of India* (1979); M. Mujeeb, *Islamic Influence on Indian Society* (1972); Tarachand, *Influence of Islam on Indian Culture* (1922); Lal, K.S., *Growth of Muslim Population in Medieval India, 1000-1800 A.D.* (1973).

The Literature of Islamic Studies can be discussed under three categories: (1) Writers; (2) Languages, and (3) Subjects/Topics.

WRITERS OF THE ISLAMIC LITERATURE

Writers on Islam include both Muslims and non-Muslims. The present desk book has included 442 experts living in India today representing both these categories. It represents the academicians (Research Guides) and non-research guides (i.e., Scholars/Authors) who have a noteworthy contribution.

Muslim Writers

The approach of Muslim Writers has been to apply and transmit Islam, as a practical way of life, as a living religion, and to project religion which not only reflects dogma, faith and belief but also extends to all walks of life in preaching and practice.

The search for original Greek and Roman sources, translation and transfer of the entire ancient, cultural and literary treasures, research into various fields, and the growth and development of various Islamic sciences and philosophies shows the approach of Muslim writers. Further, spread of Islam and Muslim culture all over Arabia and the world at large, application of the principles of *Ijtehad* and other endeavours on similar lines, also speak explicitly of the muslim approach to Islamic studies.

Moreover, learning and science possessed no votaries in pre-Islamic Arabia. Poetry, Oratory and judicial astrology were the most favoured pastime persuits. It is interesting to note that the art of writing came in Arabia only a short time before the birth of Prophet Mohammed.

Those who accepted the preachings of Prophet Mohammed and

embraced Islam received good lot of inspiration to acquire knowledge. This inspiration was acquired/obtained primarily through the revealed sources: the Latest Testament : *Quran*; and secondarily through *Hadith*.

Achievement of Arabs in science, philosophy and learning had at its base two influences (i) Islamic: *Quran* and the *Hadith* and (ii) foreign Greek, Iranian, Indian and other neighbouring cultures. The foreign influence began with translation of books to Arabic from Greek, Persian and Sanskrit.

The Muslim contribution to the literary, scientific and philosophical fields has been beautifully stated by a historian of science, Sarton, in his *Introduction to the History of Science* (1931) , as follows: "The main task of mankind was accomplished by Muslims. The greatest philosopher, al-Farabi, was a Muslim; the greatest mathematicians, Abu Kamil and Ibrahim Ibn Sinan, were Muslims, the greatest geographer and encyclopaedist, al-Masudi was still a Muslim; the greatest historian, al-Tabari, was still a Muslim". It is interesting to note that the ancient world was pre-scientific. Greeks systematised, generalised and theorised and Muslims in turn developed new methods of investigation, observation and measurement and passed this scientific spirit and method to the European world.

But the History of Muslim achievements in science, philosophy and learning came to a close with the decline of the Abbaside caliphate in thirteenth century. This spirit was kept up in the form of mere repetition of earlier achievements with no constructive and productive innovations.

Noteworthy Indian writers are Ameer Khusraw, Khwaja Syed Muhamed Gesudaraz, Babar, Faizi, Abdul Qadir Badauni, Abu Fazal, Jahangir, Shah Waliullah, Sir Syed Ahmed Khan, Shibli Naumani, Abul Kalam Azad, Sir Muhammad Iqbal, etc.

In this historical context Indians – Muslims as well as non-muslims – learnt Arabic and Persian. These languages carry quite a lot Indian documentary resources on Islamic studies. Similarly Sanskrit was studied by Muslim scholars of which few were not Indians, but they produced classical works both in Sanskrit and as translations.

Non-Muslim Writers

Approaches of non-Muslim writers to Islamic studies can be seen in their vast collections of books and articles. Their writings were based on various approaches, viz., political/religious/economic/cultural. With few exceptions their understanding of Islam and its interpretation was never recognized by the orthodox Islamists who regarded them as innovators and their writings blasphemy and inroads into the true religion. Their sincerity of interpretation and the motivation behind it have been made targets. They are accused of exploiting and charging religion to serve their ends by means of speeches, missionary propaganda, anti-Islamic polemics and various attempts such as establishment of Islamic studies departments in Universities.

They are labelled as orientalists with imperialist designs aimed at political exploitation. Besides misinterpretation, they are charged with diffusing strong doses for cultural transfer of their own ways of living and thereby spread the materialist trends: a simple example of this diffusion is the Macaulay tradition that prevails over educational system in India.

Khuda Bukhsh explains the above charges in *Contributions to the History of Islamic Civilization* (1959), "when we consider the intimate relations which existed between Muslims and Christians throughout the middle ages, we find it difficult to account for the absolutely perverse and false notions about Islam which medieval writers invented with lavish unscrupulousness and circulated with indefatigable zeal.

The discrediting of Muhammed and Islam always had the intention of influencing Christians rather than converting Muslims. The Cordoban Christian writers like Eulogius and Alber, by writing and acting for certain immediate practical purposes were important and probably decisive in the formation of the 'image' of Islam in the West.

Non-Muslim writers, mostly from the occident, wrote history of Muslim culture in the light of presupposed experiences and inclinations either towards the rightist, or, the leftist ideologies. This has been true in the case of Muslim social history, cultural history, military history philosophical history and the like.

The writings of Indian non-Muslims need to be specifically analysed. Such an analysis is not taken up here. To mention a few of the Indian writers, one need not make an indepth search, Ramakrishna's *Thus spake Prophet Muhammed (n.d.)*, Ramakrishna Rao's *Muhammad the Prophet of Islam* (1983) and *Significance of Prayer in Islam* (1986), V.D. Mahajan's *Muslim Rule in India* (1984) and *Mohammedan Dynasties*; R.C. Majumdar's *Mughal Empire* (1974), Sir Janudanath Sarkar's *Mughal Economy* (1987) and *Fall of the Mughal Empire* (1964), Iswari Prasad's *Short History of Muslim Rule in India*; B.R. Verma's *Islamic Law (1986)* and *Muslim Marriage and Dissolution* (1971); Sir Dinshah Mulla's *Principles of Mohammedan Law* (1977) and so on, are only a few of the innumerable documents produced.

LANGUAGES OF THE ISLAMIC LITERATURE

As Islam spread from Arabia to non-Arab countries, from Arabic Language belt to non-Arabic, the literature of Islamic studies too started publishing in respective languages.

However, most of the literature on Islamic studies has been in Arabic, Persian, Turkish, Urdu and in other languages of East and West. These four are recognised as primary languages of the field (see Kritzeck's *Anthology of Islamic Literature from Rise of Islam to Modern Times* (1975); Najibullah's *Islamic Literature: An Introductory History with Selections* (1963); and Annamarie Schimmel's *Islamic Literatures of India* (1973).

Arabic

Arabic literature is the expression not merely of a people or a family of elated nations, but of a whole Islamic civilization embracing at different times (including Arabs), Persians and Turks, southern and eastern Europeans, Jews, Indians, Africans and several people of central and southeast Asia.

History of Arabic literature begins with the poems and proverbs of the northern – Arabs of the 5th and 6th centuries. As for written literature before the revelation of the *Quran*, little is known.

Post-Islamic Arabic literature also called medieval literature, includes poetry, belles-letters, history and biography and technical and scientific literature. Technical and Scientific include philology, geography and travel, philosophy and science. More than all medieval period includes literature on religion, on the scripture-*Quran*, on theology, on law and so on. The literary influence of the *Quran* is incontestably enormous, and it itself is the object of a vast body of technical literature.

The medieval period of Arabic literature, roughly between 750 A.C. to 1055, has been also described as the Golden Age, which had its contributors not only from Arabs, but also from Persians, Egyptians, and Africans and equally well from Spaniards.

The modern Arabic literature emerges in 19th century due to the rise of new political, social, economic and intellectual movements. A need arose for more informative, direct and purposeful literature.

Writers of the modern period opened up European culture to their fellow Arabs and printing facilities brought a complete change. Twentieth century saw a galaxy of secularist writers. The most common outlet for prose writing was in literary journalism. Fiction and theatre have their roots only in this century in Arabic literature. Similarly, poetry had a style and convention of classical age till 1940s, and after 1940s the poets introduced greater structural variety and a wider range of experience. Indian contributors on this topic include Prof. K.A. Fariq's *A History of Arabic Literature* (1978); Zubaid Ahmad's *Contribution of India to Arabic Literature* (1945).

Persian

Persian was predominant as a language of communication in South and Central Asia, for over one thousand years. The significance of Persian literature lies in the fact that it was a medium to convey the Islamic thought to a major part of non-Arab Muslim countries. However, in Persia the language of learned continued to be Arabic.

The term Persian literature is used for Iranian literature, and is used for the literature written in the new Persian since 10th century A.D. New Persian includes the literature that emerged, much transformed in grammar, vocabulary and script (now in Arabic script) some three centuries after the Arab conquest of Iran in the mid-seventh century, when Islam became the predominant religion of Iran.

Only few fragments of literature proper have survived from Pre-Islamic and early Islamic times.

The periods for study of Persian literature are the:

(i) Classical Age (1000-1450 A.C.) and
(ii) Modern Age (1950 onwards)

Poetry has been always held to be Persian literature's outstanding glory. Arabic literature stands shoulder to shoulder with Persian literary forms like *Qasida* (or formal ode), *ghazal* (or lyric), and *mathnavi* (rhyming couplet). But what was unknown to Arabs was the *rubai* (or quatrain), which has become popular through Omer Khayyam. This form of verse was the shortest in Persian poetry.

Prose had its outlet in medicine, philosophy, theology, mysticism and other literary topics. Of all branches of prose writing, history has been the most popular, and had its support even from kings and princes. The extensive historical literature is supplemented by many biographical and geographical works.

The main centre of Persian literature was transferred to India during the Safavid period (1501-1736). In India Persian material emerged in large quantity, comprising both poetical and prose works. This Indo-Persian literature evolved a tradition which continued down to this century. Indian courts encouraged and patronised literary scholarship. Equally important is the support received from *Sufis* in the development of this tradition.

Western influences were increasingly felt in the thought and demand for social and constitutional reform. This period produced scholars who could edit the Persian classics and bring out constantly original writings. Innovations included the emergence of journalism, a preference for prose, and simplification of poetry. The advances made in press and printing have also made impact on modern literary movement. (See also Wahhajuddin Ahmed's Urdu translation of Browne's *History of Persian Literature* (1936); Munibur Rahman's *Anthology of Modern Persian Poetry* (1962); and also *Anthology of Persian Poetry* (1962); Maulvi Abdul Huq's *Influence of Persian on the Marathi Language* (1935).

Turkish

Turkish was the official language of the Ottoman Empire (1300-1924). This empire, being the largest Muslim empire, Turkish language has a very significant contribution to Islamic literature. It also adopted Arabic script. Even in Turkey the language of the learned continued to be Arabic. The common feature, thus, in Persian and Turkish literature was the existence of a language and literature, influenced by Arabic in script and in communication process.

The history of Turkish literature has two periods, first period is

Islamic and the second is the modern period.

Poetry had its firm grounds in the literature of this period. A change came in poets by 10th century when they developed a classical poetry of their own, by thoroughly assimilating the Persian art poetique and imposing upon it their own personal characteristics. The prose of this period is mainly represented by historians mostly by translations of religious or popular stories and semiepic accounts of battles.

Within the Islamic period lies the classical period ranging in between 15th century and 17th century. By 19th century commences the modern period which came under western influence. The other features of this period are development of independent trends in literary fields and eruption of full-fledged secular society and with it the secular literature of 1920 onwards.

Urdu

Urdu is an Indian language which has a wealth of Islamic literature, comparable to any other Islamic language. We have translations of almost all major works on Islamic literature in Urdu from Arabic, Persian and other languages.

The word 'Urdu' is derived from the Turkish word '*ordu*' which is the root of the English word 'Horde' meaning army or crowd. There are various theories about the origin of the name, and above-mentioned is one. Urdu has also been called Hindustani, *Urdu-e-Moalla*, etc. Urdu is written in Perso-Arabic script. As contrasted with Hindi which drew its inspiration from Sanskrit and Hindu culture, Urdu looked to Persian literature for motifs and forms to the Islamic faith for its enrichment.

The origins of Urdu literature date back to the period of Ghaznavi rule in Punjab in 12th century. Urdu verses have been identified in Amir Khusraw's (1253-1325 AC) writings. Urdu literature gradually evolved two dialectical growth, viz. literary South Indian and elegant North Indian. These were interfused with Aurangzeb's (1618-1707) conquest of Deccan.

Since Urdu had its association with urban environment, its prose, poetry and other literary forms had more urban look and has better standing than the folk literature.

It was by mid-19th century that the novel was introduced to Urdu literature, under the influence of western literature. Similar is the history of Urdu drama. The plays tried to demonstrate socio-moral aspects. Poetical forms were used by Hali, Iqbal, etc. to bring social-moral revolution. (See Abdul Hai, *Islami Ulum Wa Funun Hindustan Mein* (1974); Grahm T. Bailay, *Hindustani* (1952); Din Mohammed, *Hindustani* (1933); Nizamuddin Gorekar's *Glimpses of Urdu Literature* (1961); Shawkat Sabzwari, *Dastan-e-Zaban-e-Urdu* (1965); Mohammed Sadiq, *History of Urdu Literature* (1984) and Ziaul Islam, *Glimpses of Modern Urdu Literature* (1949).

Thus, the Islamic literature has appeared in different languages. This dispersion of literature in languages of East and West is a well-known fact.

SUBJECT TOPICS OF ISLAMIC LITERATURE

This subject-content can be studied under two different perspectives: (i) Literary and (ii) Philosophical or Ideal structure of Islamic studies.

Literary

Islam has been studied in two ways : (a) faith and (b) practice or (a) as a religion and (b) as a way of life.

Faith or religion includes topics like the *Quran* and *Quranic* literature, the *Hadith* and *Hadith* literature, Biography of the Prophet Mohammed, and his companions, theology, etc.

The *Quran* is the revealed source for guidance of humanity. It is originally in Arabic, and has been translated into most of the languages of the world. There have been several commentaries of *Quran* from time to time. Depending on the inclination of the commentator these commentaries treat the subject on the basis of tradition, history philosophy, linguistics, law, etc.

Of all the prophets and great personalities of the world, the life of Prophet Muhammed stands in full light of history covering all aspects of his life and teachings. The traditional literature, called the '*Hadith*' in Arabic terminology means what the Prophet said and did. The authenticity of the traditions, has been studied, checked and verified as no other historical material has ever been. The traditions have been compiled in various series by different traditionalists, called *Muhaddithun* in Arabic.

In the sphere of every day life, a Muslim has to observe, besides the regular rituals, his duties to fellow beings. This subject has been enlarged upon by the traditionalists and jurists. It encompasses the whole range of man's duties to his parents, family, friends, neighbours and to all humanity as well as to the animals. With the development of human knowledge several inter-disciplinary and multi-disciplinary branches have come into existence, viz., Islamic economics, Islamic sociology, Islamic politics, Geopolitics of Muslim countries, Islamic psychology and Islamic medicine.

For example, Islamic economics has vast material for study and research based on the *Quran*, the *Hadith*, history, sociology, psychology, and philosophy. The *Quran* prescribes the ways of accumulations and distribution of wealth. The *Hadith* elaborates them. Sociologically the distribution of wealth according to Islam is neither capitalistic nor socialistic. Psychologically it is motivating the haves to share with have-nots. Philosophically it prepares the mind to sacrifice rather than exploit and to serve for the betterment of the society. Politically, under international economic relations, it sets the framework for a better world government, and coexistence of human beings. Islamic economics comprises the following concepts among others : taxation (*zakath*), charities, endowments, banks (*Bait-ul-Mal*), interest in its various forms : like simple and compound; natural resources, income and expenditure, and budgeting and planning.

PHILOSOPHICAL OR IDEA STRUCTURE OF ISLAMIC STUDIES

The structure of Islamic studies can also be seen in the world's first classification schemes of knowledge given by celebrated Muslim scholars. The schemes they propounded maintained distinction between revealed knowledge and experimental sciences. This distinction was essential to keep sciences away from magic and miracles, to save Islam from credulity, superstition and pseudo-religious observation, and primarily this distinction was aimed at giving a human face to science and technology. (See Ziauddin Sardar, *Islam : Outline of a Classification Scheme* (1979).

One of the first attempts to classify knowledge was made by al-Kindi (801-873 AC). It was, infact, al-Farabi (d. 950) who produced one of the most used and widely influential schemes, and is summarised under the following groups : (i) science of language, (ii) logic, (iii) propaedutic sciences, (iv) science of nature, and (v) science of society.

The above five groups indicate the level of understanding about knowledge, as far back as the 10th century and as comprehended by an eminent philosopher. One group can be described in detail, showing its sub-categories as given by al-Farabi.

Propaedutic Sciences

(a) Arithmetic: practical, theoretical;
(b) Geometry : practical, theoretical;
(c) Optics;
(d) Science of heavens : astronomy-motions and figures of the heavenly bodies;
(e) Music : practical, theoretical;
(f) Science of weights; and
(g) Science of tool-making.

As different sciences expanded, classification schemes became broader and more detailed. Ibn Sina (980-1037) and al-Ghazali (1058-1111), further extended al-Farabi's scheme of classification.

However, the greatest personality in this area of knowledge classification is that of Ibn Khaldun (1332-1406) who outlined a scheme of classification on two distinct themes, viz., Shariah Sciences and Philosophical Sciences. While former deals with Islamic law and religion, and the latter deals with those subjects acquired by reflection, experimentation, experience and observation.

The following is the broad outline of his scheme:

1. Shariah Sciences are transmitted sciences going back ultimately to the origin of Revelation:

   (a) The *Quran*, its interpretation and recitation;
   (b) The *Hadith*, study of the text and the chain of narrators;
   (c) Jurisprudence;
   (d) Linguistic sciences, such as grammar, lexicography and literature; and
   (e) Sufism.

2. Philosophical Sciences:

   (a) Logic;
   (b) Natural sciences: physics, medicine, mechanics, agriculture, alchemy;
   (c) Sciences dealing with quantity : geometry (plain and spherical optics), arithmetic (including algebra) music, astronomy; and
   (d) Paranormal sciences: magic, talisman, occult, etc.

Contemporary scene shows existence of important schemes of classification, like Dewey Decimal Classification (DDC), Universal Decimal Classification (UDC), Library of Congress Classification (LC), Bibliographical Classification (BC), and Colon Classification (CC). These schemes help in classification of books, articles, reports and other informational material on Islam and Muslims. A glance at these schemes, however indicates that these lack a provision for accurate subject representation and are essentially "West-oriented" schemes.

In his proposed scheme, Ziauddin Sardar has 16 main classes viz., Islam, the *Quran*, the *Hadith*, Prophet Muhammed, Muslim faith, Philosophy, *Ibadah*, Politics, Law, Economics, Education and Learning, History of people, Civilization and Culture, *Ummah*, Human behavioural characteristics, contemporary issues.

Based on the above discussion on writers, language and subjects/topics of the literature of Islamic studies, it can be safely concluded that the structure of Islamic studies is a unity in diversity.

RESEARCH IN ISLAMIC STUDIES

Till recently research on Islamic studies has been mostly on Islam as a religion rather than as a way of life. Research has been done on a wide variety, on religious belief, faith. practices, principles, morals, etc. Research has of late been also on Islam as a way of life and as such there is growing attraction towards inter-disciplinary and multi-disciplinary aspects.

There are many research centres in India on Islamic studies both at Universities and in research organizations. The University Departments, usually full-fledged, carry on a study and research programme. All universities in India and abroad do not designate the departments concerned with Islamic studies, uniformly with a single name. The Indian samples are – Arab Culture, West Asian Studies, Middle Eastern Studies, Religious Studies, Comparative Religion, Arabic, Persian and Urdu. The research organisations in India and elsewhere are run by private agencies, semi-government agencies or government agencies.

The Indian examples of the private bodies are *Madrasas* and Institutes of Islamic Studies etc., and Indian Council of Historical Research, Asiatic Society, Indian Council of Social Science Research, etc., represent Government or Semi-Government bodies.

A detailed background of the various departments catering to this area of studies is available in Yusufuddin's *Oriental and Islamic Studies in World Universities* (1953). This source carries description of syllabus of study in the institutions, its main and subsidiary papers, optionals (electives) offered, research and study, incentives and facilities, etc.

The present book enlists 175 centres of learning Islamic languages and literatures; 156 centres (Departments) in Universities and Colleges: 62 private bodies devoted to study and research, and 38 funding/supporting agencies.

OVERLAPS AND INTERLINKS

This pertains to the links and overlaps in relation to inter-disciplinary and multi-disciplinary studies. The list of 442 doctoral theses in this book clearly state this significant feature of Islamic studies.

It is apt to mention that there has been an interest in comparative religious studies since long. The Emperor Akbar had a regular programme each day for religious discourse and dialogue. In today's study circles, the theosophists have a similar gathering. Overlapping will be the direct resultant in comparative studies. For instance, this can be visualised in Islamic Sociology, Islamic Jurisprudence, or, Islamic Political System, or, Theo-Democratic Political system of Islamic Polity. Interlinks can be demonstrated in Inter-disciplinary and multi-disciplinary studies. For instance, politics has various meanings and so also political systems. Interlinks are necessary to explain the contemporary Muslim political experience and compare it up with the non-Muslim political experiences and evolve out some generalisations.

Similar interlinks and overlaps can be found in a topic like Eastern Religious, or Eastern Culture or Eastern Spiritualism. For example, mysticism is a common subject of the East and this studied with different religio-political backgrounds enables one to see the trends and future prospects. These interlinks and overlaps indicate the vastness of the area of Islamic studies. In this context it is significant to mention that Islamic studies can be studied under Humanities, Social Sciences and Science, and as such overlaps and interlinks are unavoidable.

Current Environment

Islamic studies has today different focus for different groups of the world. Both the capitalists and communists seek the subject with political motives. The Christian missionaries have slightly modified their approach that existed till the end of 19th century. Now they do not speak much critically, instead try to prove that Christianity is 'the' way of life, and this message is carried on through the term 'dialogue'. For the Jews vital is the question of widening the boundaries of the sacred land and hence to motivate their own people they approach Islamic studies in a negative sense.

Research on Islam is more than ever wanting. Awareness of Islam and Muslims, though superficial, has considerably increased while more and more people are misinformed, and the bias towards anything and everything relating to Islam and Muslims is multiplying.

It is interesting to note that even non-Muslim elite have very vague idea of Islam and Muslims. They associate Islam with Khomeni, petro-dollars, oil and more often with Arabs and Arab culture, which may ironically vary from Arab Christians to Arab Jews. Literature on the Muslim countries carries only political themes. Muslims or Islam rarely find a place in non-Muslim publications. Edward Said's *Orientalism* (1978) has many such specimens.

Coming to the internal sources, there is again a good deal of difference of focus. Few Muslim groups emphasize the spiritual life (like the *Sufis*) and are least concerned with day to day events and chores, some are moderate (like the *Jammatis*) who try to balance between the matter and spirit, and few others are the materialists (like the *Ahl-e-Hadith*), who have least thought on spirituality. Further within the Islamic fold, there is an increase of such groups and minds who give a public call for return to the principles of Islam.

Prof. Montgomery Watt, is of the opinion that a call to return to roots of Islam, is "basically sound". He defends this return as an essential feature to combat the challenge of materialism, unemployment, growing economic strains and political exploitations.

As against those who dubbed this return to roots as resurgence, or as some called it upsurge, Barakat Ahmad (former Member of the Indian Foreign Service) says "Bad times have visited the Muslims before and Muslim thinkers, scholars, divines and soldiers have always stood up to save the *Ummah* (the Muslim Community) either from stagnation, invasion or internal decay". "Crusaders ravaged the world of Islam", he adds convincingly, "from 1096 to 1204". The Mongols sacked Baghdad in 1258. In 1492 Arabs were expelled from Spain after 700 years of enlightened rule. In 1759 Nadir Shah looted Delhi, in 1857 the Mughals lost their nominal Kingdom of Delhi, and finally in 1918 the Ottoman empire "disintegrated and vanished" in 1926.

> "The non-Muslim powers outside as well as the un-Islamic forces inside have been alerted, rather alarmed, by this nemesis, and these powers and forces are afraid", says Abdul Moghani, "that their political hegemony and economic monopoly will be broken" initially in the third world and followed by a similar break in "first and second worlds of Europe and America".

Dissemination

This aspect requires discussion under topics like conferences and publications. Conference covers in its perview all meetings, discussions, workshops, seminars and lectures.

There have been umpteen conferences in and outside the Muslim world. The conference of Orientalists is a perennial feature. Lectures and seminars go round the year and help in discussing the vital issues.

Extensive lectures go almost as a daily feature in various parts of the Muslim world, conducted by the Universities and Muslim Seminaries (*Madrasas*). Extensive lectures have been a traditional pattern and mostly are part of continuing education. The topics cover a wide range of subjects, which are heavily dominated by spiritualism. These lectures at times take the shape of adult education to teach the fundamentals and principles of Islam and Islamic way of living, and what is disseminated through this programme is rarely recorded and communicated to others.

Publications concerning Islamic literature appear in a wide variety of ephemeral and non-ephemeral sources. It is difficult to know what all is published, where and when. The copyright provision and enactment does exist in India. Yet most of the publications in the world do not get into the national and international bibliographical sources. Thousands of books on Islam are being regularly published, in various languages and not a single source has succeeded in covering the entire material at least in one language. This Directory has listed some recent in-print references and sources.

There are no less than 100 research/non-research Journals on Islam in various languages and there is no single source to enlist the details of place of publication, frequency, address, subscription, etc. Pamphlets, reports, reviews, are the other sources which carry material on Islamic studies.

Publications of primary material have increased tremendously, but the growth of secondary sources which could have indexed and abstracted this primary literature have not been proportional. This is an alarming issue. The Indian indexes have failed in covering even one-fourth of the publications of Islamic studies.

There are many libraries in India on Islamic studies. Zubair Ahmed's *Islami Kutub Khane* (1961) gives a background of the medieval libraries in India. The Directory under consideration has listed three types of libraries:

(a) 19 government libraries managed or aided;
(b) 15 University libraries which have significant collections; and
(c) 37 private libraries.

There are many publishers, distributors and book-sellers in the country. This book has 51 non-commercial (or non-profit), 88 commercial and 36 renowned general agencies with interest in Islamic studies.

For access and control of Islamic studies literature there is a lack of coordination among writers, producers, distributors and libraries. There are no national level documentation centres and libraries. The entire scene needs review and planning to meet the live demands of today and to foresee a vision of tomorrow.

2. DOCUMENTS/INFORMATION

Reference Books (Current)
Journals
Completed Doctoral Research
Cities of Historical Importance

REFERENCE BOOKS (CURRENT)

Comprehensive Works

Abidi, Sartaj A. and S.K. Sharma (1974). Fifty Years of Indian History Writings. Index of Articles in *Journal of Indian History*. V. 1-50 (1921/22-1972). New Delhi: Gitanjali Prakashan.

Dalvi, Muhammad Abdur-rahim (1989). *1400 Years of Islam: A Deskbook*, Pune: Muhammad Dalvi Wakf.

Hai, M.A. (1984). *Handbook of Islam*. Delhi: Maktaba Alhasnat.

Haroon, Mohammed (1987). *Cataloguing of Indian Muslim Names*. Delhi: Indian Bibliographies Bureau.

Nadvi, S. Abdul Hasan Ali (1983). *Islamic Studies, Orientalists and Muslim Scholars*. Lucknow: Academy of Islamic Research & Publications.

Siddiqui, M. Suleman and M. Ahmadullah (1984). *Index of Islamic Culture: Subject, Author and Reviews, 1927–1980*. Hyderabad Islamic Culture Board.

Arts

Chandra, Jagdish (1978). *Bibliography of Indian art, history and archaeology* (Dr. Anand K. Coomaraswamy memorial volume, Vol. 1: Indian art) Delhi: Delhi Printers Prakashan.

Desai, Ziauddin (1971). *Mosques of India*. New Delhi: Publications Division, Ministry of Information and Broadcasting.

Fehervari, G. and Y.H. Safdari (1981). *1400 years of Islamic Art: A descriptive catalogue*. London: Khalili Gallery.

Hingorani, R.P. (1976). *Painting in South Asia: A Bibliography*. Varanasi: Bharatiya Publishing House.

Islamic Heritage of India (1986). New Delhi: National Museum.

Salar Jung Museum (1986). *Journeys in Art through the Salar Jung Museum*. Hyderabad: Salar Jung Museum Board.

Smart, E. and D.S. Walker (1986). *Pride of the Princes: Indian Art of the Mughal Era in the Cincinnati Art Museum*. Cincinnati; Ohio: Cincinnati Art Museum.

Titley, Norah M. (1977). *Miniatures from Persian Manuscripts. A catalogue and subject index of paintings from Persia, India and Turkey in the British library and the British Museum*. British Museum Publications Ltd. for British library.

Bio-Bibliographies

General

Cutchi Memon Jamat of Andhra Pradesh (1986). Directory of Members. Secunderabad.

Eminent Mussalmans (1981). New Delhi: Neeraj Publishing House, (rpt.)

Haroon, Mohamed (1989). *Muslims of India: Their Literature on Education, History, Politics, Religion, Socio-Economic and Communal Problems*. New Delhi: Indian Bibliographies Bureau.

Indian Council of Social Science Research, Southern Regional Centre (1983). *Hyderabad: Select Bibliography of Indian Muslims*.

Jain, N.K. (1978). *Biographical Dictionary of Muslims in the Indian Subcontinent, 1957–1976*. Columbia: South Asia Books.

—. (1980). ed. *Muslims in India: A Biographical Dictionary* V. 1 (A-J) New Delhi: Manohar Publications.

—. (1983). ed. *Muslims in India: A Biographical Dictionary*. V. 2 (K-Z) New Delhi: Manohar Publications.

Khan, S. Ali (1981). *History and Historians of Rajasthan*. Delhi: Triveni.

Kumedan, B.S. (1978). *Modernisation and Social Reforms among the Muslims: A Select Bibliography*. Delhi: Delhi School of Social Work.

Poonawala, Ismail K. (1977). *Bibliography of Ismaili Literature*. Malibu: Undena Publication.

Shakir, Moin (1974). *Muslim Attitude: A Trend Report and Bibliography*. Aurangabad: Parimal Prakashan.

Satyaprakash (1984). *Muslims in India: A Bibliography of their Religious, Socio-Economic and Political Literature*. Gurgaon: Indian Documentation Service.

Individual

Abul Kalam Azad, Nizami, Khaliq Ahmed (1988): *Maulana Azad Album* (Urdu with English translation) New Delhi: D.K. Publishers, Distributors.

Abul Raihan al-Biruni. Khan, A. Saeed, Comp. (1982). *Bibliography of the works of Abul Raihan al-Biruni*. New Delhi: I.N.S.A.

Khan-i-Khanan Khan, I. Alam (1973). *Political Biography of a Mughal Noble Munim Khan Khan-i-Khanan*. New Delhi: Oriental Publications.

Mirza Asadullah Khan Shahib, Ghalib Academy (1970). *Ghalib Bibliography*. New Delhi.

Sir Shaikh Mohammed Iqbal Azhar, Malik Mueen Nawaz (1978). *A Bibliography of articles on Iqbal (1900–1977)*. Lahore: Islamic Book Service.

Theses on Iqbal, Rizvi, Syed Jamil Ahmad (1977). *A Bibliographical survey of the theses on Iqbal* submitted to the University of the Punjab. Lahore, 1950–1976. Lahore: Aziz.

Usmani, M. Adil and Nasim Fatima (1977). *Books on Allama Iqbal in University Libraries of Pakistan: Allama Iqbal birth centenary celebrations: 1977*. Karachi: Karachi University (Karachi University Library publications).

Sir Syed Ahmed Khan, Aligarh Muslim University. Maulana Azad Library (1971). *Sir Syed Ahmed Khan. A select bibliography*. Aligarh.

Sayyid Ahmad Khan: Bibliography, Nizami, Khaliq A. (1974). Delhi: Publications Division.

Askari, Syed H. (1985). *Collected Works of Prof. Syed Hasan Askari*. Patna: Khuda Bhaksh Oriental Public Library.

Directories

Desai, Ziyauddin (1978). *Centres of Islamic learning in India*. Delhi: Publications Division, Ministry of Information and Broadcasting.

Jaffar, Saiyid Mohammad (1971). *Comp. Research Facilities in Uttar Pradesh, Gurgaon*, Haryana: Indian Documentation Service.

Sastry, P.P. Subramanya (1970). *Descriptive catalogue of the Islamic manuscripts in the Govt. Oriental Manuscripts Library*, Madras. 5 V. Govt. of Madras.

History

General

Aziz, K.K. (1972). *All India Muslim Conference, 1928–1935: A Documentary Record.* Karachi: National Publishing House.

Dogra, R.C. (1988). *Catalogue of the Early Printed Books on South Asia: From 1586 to 1864 held in the Library of Oriental and African Studies*, London New Delhi: Aditya Prakashan.

Gurney, Gene (1986). *Kingdoms of Asia, the Middle East and Africa: An Illustrated Encyclopaedia of Ruling Monarchs from Ancient Times to the Present.* New York: Crown.

Khan, Shafaat A. (1986). *Sources for the study of British India in the 17th century.* Delhi: Pankaj Publications.

Sharma, Jagdish N. (1974). *Sources of Indian Civilization: A Bibliography of works by World Orientalists, other than Indians.* New Delhi: Vikas.

Deccan

Ayyangar, S. Krishnaswamy ed. (1986). *Sources of Vijayanagar History* Delhi: Gyan Publishing House.

Henderson, Jr. (1987). *Coins of Haidar Ali and Tipu Sultan.* Delhi: D.K. Publishers and Distributors.

Khalidi, Omar (1987). *Dakan (Deccan) Under the Sultans 1296–1724: A Bibliography of Monographic and Periodical Literature. Wichita*, K.S.: Hyderabad Historical Society.

—. (1987). *Hyderabad State under the Nizams, 1724–1948: A Bibliography of Monographic and Periodical literature.* Wichita: Hyderabad Historical Society.

Khan, M.A. Wali (1980). *Copper Coins of Adil Shah Dynasty of Bijapur, Hyderabad*: Birla Archaeological and Cultural Research Institute.

Mughals

Andhra Pradesh (India) State archives (1980). *Mughal Documents: Catalogue of Aurangzeb's Reign.* ed. & comp. by M.A. Nayeem, V.1 Pt.1, Hyderabad.

Marshall, D.N. (1985). *Mughals in India: A Bibliographical Survey of Manuscripts*. London: Mansell.

Rodgers, C.J. (1985). *Catalogue of the Coins: The Coins of the Mughal Emperors of India* in 4 Vols. New Delhi: D.K. Publishers, Distributors. (rpt.)

Rajasthan

Desai, Ziauddin (1971). *Published Muslim Inscriptions of Rajasthan* Jaipur, Directorate of Archaeology and Museums.

Sepoy Mutiny

India, National Archives (1970). *Descriptive list of Mutiny Papers in the National Archives of India*. Bhopal. V. 3. Delhi: Manager of Publications.

Islamic Jurisprudence (Fiqh)

Islahi, M. Yusuf (1986). *Everyday Fiqh*. Tr. Abdul Aziz Kalam. New Delhi: Adam.

Literatures

General

Schimmel, A. (1973). *Islamic literatures of India* (History of Indian literature Series, V. 7), Wiesbaden: Otto Harrasowitz.

Arabic

Ashraf, Muhammad (1981). *A concise descriptive catalogue of the Arabic manuscripts in the Salar Jung Museum and Library*. Volume IV: Concerning 448 manuscripts of Islamic Theology. Hyderabad: Salar Jung Museum and Library (Salar Jung Museum and Library Publications, new series 10/4).

Asiatic Society (1980) *Catalogue of Arabic Manuscripts in Tabular* Form. Prepared by K.M. Maitra. Rev. and ed. by M.S. Khan Calcutta.

Khan, S. Ali (1983). *Catalogue of the Arabic Manuscripts: Prayers, dialectics, al-fiqh and law of inheritance.* V. 2, Tonk: Arabic & Persian Research Institute (A.P.R.I. Pub. Series 9).

—. (1980). *Catalogue of the Arabic Manuscripts:* Quranic *Sciences and Science of Traditions.* V.1, Tonk: Arabic & Persian Research Institute.

Persian

Hillmann, Michael C. (1976). Twentieth *Century Persian literature in translation: A Bibliography.* Cultural Department, Imperial Embassy of Iran (Washington).

Khan, S. Ali (1986). *Descriptive catalogue of the Persian Manuscripts.* Tonk: Arabic and Persian Research Institute.

Razi, F.D. (1981). *Modern Persian Dictionary (Persian-Urdu-English)*, New Delhi: Kitab Bhavan.

Urdu

George, K.M. (1983). *Comparative Indian Literature.* 2 V. Trivandrum: Kerala Sahitya Academy.

Haq. Abdul ed. (1989). *Practical Advanced Twentieth Century Dictionary: English into English and Urdu.* Delhi : Arjun Book Depot (student edition).

—. (1988), *Practical Standard Twentieth Century Dictionary: Urdu into English.* Delhi: Arjun Book Depot (student edition).

—. (1975), *Standard English-Urdu Dictionary.* Delhi: J.S. Sant Singh and Sons.

Qadir, Abdul (1977), *Famous Urdu Poets and Writers* ed. 2. New Delhi: Seemant Prakashan.

Minorities

Motamar al-Alam al-Islami (1977). *Country by Country outline survey of Muslim Minorities of the World.* Karachi.

Sharma, Jagdish N. (1977). *India's Minorities: A Bibliographical Study.* New Delhi: Vikas.

Skyhawk, High Van ed. (1986). *Minorities on Themselves* (South Asian Digest of Regional Writing, V. 2). Stuttgart: Steiner Verlag.

Muslim Women

Kabir, Kausar and Inamul Kabir (1983). *Biographical Dictionary of Prominent Muslim Ladies*. New Delhi: Light & Life Publishers.

Yaqin, Anwarul and Badar Anwar (1982). *Protection of Women under the law: An Annotated Bibliography*. New Delhi: Deep and Deep.

Philosophy

Shaikh, M.S. (1970) *Dictionary of Muslim Philosophy.*

Political Science

Aziz, K.K. (1986), *Muslims under Congress Rule, 1937–1939: A Documentary Record*, 2 V. Delhi: Renaissance.

Habib, Irfan (1982). *Atlas of the Mughal Empire: Political and economic maps with detailed notes, bibliography and index.* Aligarh: Aligarh Muslim University.

Khan, A. Mohammed (1985). *Medieval Gujarat: Its Political and Statistical History based on Mirat-i-Ahmadi*. Tr. James Bird. Delhi: Indian Bibliographies Bureau.

Tyagi, K.G. (1984). *Foreign Researches on Indian Political Systems and Processes*. Delhi: Pinka Agencies.

Zaidi, A. Momin (1987), *Muslim School of Congress: The Political Ideas of Muslim Congress Leaders from Badruddin Tayyabji to Maulana Abul Kalam Azad, 1885–1947*. New Delhi: Indian Institute of Applied Political Research.

Quran

Aneesuddin, Mir (1988). *Index to the Holy Quran*. Hyderabad: Islamic Academy of Sciences.

Binark, I. and L. Eren (1987). *World Bibliography of Translations of the Meanings of the Holy* Quran: *Printed Translations, 1515–1980.* London: Keagen Paul International.

Husain, Ashraf (1986). *Record of all the* Quranic *and Non-Historical Epigraphs on the Protected Monuments in the Delhi Province*. New Delhi: Manager of Publications.

Kheirie, Alhaj Khan Bahadur, A.A. (1988). *Index-cum-concordance for the Holy Quran*. New Delhi: Kitab Bhavan.

Rahman Afzal-ur (1987), *Subject index of the Holy Quran*. New Delhi: Noor Publishing House.

Research Work

Inter-university Board of India (1979). Bibliography of Doctoral dissertations accepted by Indian Universities, 1857–1970. New Delhi. 5 V.

National Register of Doctoral Dissertations accepted and in progress in Social Science and Humanities in Indian Universities. (1980). Bhopal: Council of Oriental Research. 2 pts.

Rajannan, Busnagi, ed. (1981). South Indian Studies: Abstracts of American Doctoral dissertations relating to South India. Salem: Institute of Kongu Studies.

Rothermund, D. (1975). *Islam in South Asia: A Survey of Current Research*. London: Steiner, Franz.

Science And Technology

Rahman, A. (1982). *Science and Technology in Medieval India: A Bibliography of Source Materials in Sanskrit, Arabic and Persian*. New Delhi: Indian National Academy.

Other Related Sources

Directory of Publishers and Booksellers in India (1986). New Delhi: New light.

Gidwani, N.N. and K. Navalani (1974). *Guide to Reference Material on India*. Jaipur: Saraswati Pub. 2 V.

India: Who's Who, 1988-89 (1989). 19th ed. New Delhi: INFA.

Indian Books in Print, 1988 (1988). New Delhi: Indian Bibliographies Bureau, 3 V.

Jain, M.K. (1989). *Indiana: A Bibliography of Bibliographical Sources*. New Delhi: Concept.

Khan, M.A. Shaheed (1983). *Directory of Islamic libraries and librarians*. California: Islamic library Association.

Singh, Mohinder (1975). *Comp. Learned societies and institutions in India, activities and publications.* Including over 4,000 research oriented titles. Delhi: Metropolitan Book.

Who's Who of Indian Writers, 1983 (1983). New Delhi: Sahitya Akademy.

JOURNALS

Primary Journals

Albaas-el-Islami (Arabic), P.B. 93, Nadva, Lucknow. 226007, (U.P.)

Annals of Oriental Research, University of Madras, Madras-600005, (T.N.)

Ashrafia (Urdu), Mubarakpur, Azamgarh-276404, (U.P.)

Bulletin Christian Institute of Islamic Studies, Henry Martin Institute of Islamic Studies, P.B. 153, Hyderabad-500001, (A.P.)

Bulletin of the Institute of Islamic Studies, Institute of Islamic Studies, Aligarh Muslim University, Aligarh-202001, (U.P.)

Bulletin Ramakrishna Mission Institute of Culture, Gol Park, Calcutta-700029, (W.B.)

Al-Burhan (Urdu), Urdu Bazar, Delhi-110006.

Al-Daie (Arabic), Darul Uloom Deoband, Deoband-247554, (U.P.)

Al-Furqan (Urdu), Lucknow-226001. (U.P.)

Indian Philosophical Quarterly, Department of Philosophy, University of Poona, Pune-411007. (Maharashtra).

Indo-Iranaica, 12, Dr. M. Ishaqne Road, Calcutta-799916. (W.B.)

Islam Aur Asr-e-Jadeed (Urdu) Jamia Nagar, New Delhi-110025.

Islam and Comparative Law Quarterly, Indian Insittute of Islamic Studies, New Delhi-110062.

Islam and the Modern Age, Jamia Nagar, New Delhi-110025.

Islam Culture, Islamia Culture Board, Hyderabad-500007. (A.P.)

Islamic Perspectives, Institute of Islamic Studies, Irene College, 2nd floor, 4th Road, Santacruz (East) Bombay-400055. (Maharashtra).

Jamia (Urdu) Jamia Nagar, New Delhi-110025.

Journal of Objective Studies, Editor, 4/1707, Muzammil Manzil Complex, A.D.M. Road, Aligarh-202001. (U.P.).

Journal of Oriental Research, Sastri Research Institute, Mylapore, Madras-600004. (T.N.).

Khuda Bakhsh Library Journal, Khuda Bakhsh O.P. Library, Patna-800004. (Bihar).

Kitab Numa (Urdu) Maktaba Jamia Ltd., Jamia Nagar, New Delhi-110025.

MAAS Journal of Islamic Sciences, Faridi House, 51, Syed Nagar, Aligarh-202001. (U.P.)

Maarif (Urdu), Darul Musannifeen, Azamgarh-276001. (U.P.)

Monthly Jameatur Rashad (Urdu) Azamgarh-276001. (U.P.)

Muslim India, 8, Feroze Shah Road, New Delhi-110001.

Muslim India (Urdu), 1846, Kalan Mahal, Delhi-110006.

Nawa-e-Adab, (Urdu), Anjuman-e-Islam Urdu Research Institute, 92, D.N. Road, Bombay-400001. (Maharashtra)

Nida-e-Milat, Lucknow, (U.P.)

Oriental Institute Journal, Tilak Road, Opp. Sayaji Ganj Tower, P.B. 75, Baroda-390002. (Gujarat)

Al-Raid, Lucknow. (U.P.)

Al Rashad (Urdu) Azamgarh-276001. (U.P.)

Religion and Society, Christian Institute for Study of Religion and Society, P.O. Box 4600, 17, Millers Road, Bangalore-560046. (Karnataka)

Safa (Urdu) Darul Uloom Sabeelussalam, Balapur, Hyderabad-500005. (A.P.)

Sidq-e-Jadid (Urdu), Lucknow. (U.P.)

Studies in Islam, Indian Institute of Islamic Studies, Tughluqabad, New Delhi-110062.

Taamir-e-Hayat (Urdu), Nadwa, Lucknow-226007. (U.P.)

Tahqeeqat-e-Islami, Aligarh-202001. (U.P.)

Thought, Siddhartha Publications. 35, Netaji Subhash Marg, Delhi-110006.

Other Journals

Afkar-e-Milli (Urdu), E22/153, Zakir, Jamia Nagar, New Delhi-110025.

Arannam (Women's monthly) (Malayalam) Silver Hills, Calicut-673012. (Kerala)

Crescent Times, 37/2864/D, Thoufeeque Bldg., Market Road, Cochin-682031. (Kerala)

Daee (Urdu) 206, E.R. Road, Bombay-400003. (Maharashtra)

Dalit Voice, 109/7th Cross, Palace Lower, Orchards, Bangalore-560003. (Karnataka)

Dawat, 1525, Suwale, New Delhi-110002.

Al Faisal (Urdu), 3-6-373/A, Himayat Nagar, Hyderabad-500029. (A.P.)

Farogh-e-Urdu, 37, Ameenabad Park, Lucknow-226001. (U.P.)

Geethurai Weekly, Lakkad Kot, Hyderabad-500002. (A.P.)

Hayat Nao, Jamiatul Falah, Balereaganj, Azamgarh-276001. (U.P.)

Al Hind Al-Arab Magazine, Ali Cottage, Mukarram Jahi Road, Hyderabad-500001. (A.P.)

Humanizer, Kazi-Kadil, P.O. Habbakada, Srinagar-190001. (J & K)

Islamic Review, 361/29, 11th Cross, 2nd Block, Jayanagar, Bangalore-560011. (Karnataka)

Islamic Voice, 64, Richmond Road, Bangalore-560025. (Karnataka)

Islamic World, CB/2-D1, Munirka Scheme, Phase-3, New Delhi-110067.

Kanthi (Hindi) 1525, Suiwalan, New Delhi-110002.

Khabarnama, (Urdu), U.P. Urdu Akademi, Qaiser Bagh, Lucknow-226001. (U.P.)

Lahren (Urdu), Adabi Sangam, Md. Ali Jauhar Marg, Jamia Nagar, New Delhi-110025.

Madhyamam Daily (Malayalam), Ideal Publications Trust, Calicut-673012. (W.B.)

Mahanama-e-Fankar (Urdu) Lakkad Kot, Hyderabad-500002. (A.P.)

Majmooae Akhbare Sadaquat (Urdu) Imambada Compound, Synagouge Street, Pune-411001. (Maharashtra)

Malarvadi (Malayalam) Children's Monthly, Silver Hills, Calicut-673012. (Kerala)

Meezan, 21 (Bengali), Lenin Sarani, Calcutta-700001. (W.B.)

Mujahid (Assamese). Guwahati-781001. (Assam)

Munsif (Urdu) Daily. P.O.B. 363, Nampally Station Road, Hyderabad-500001. (A.P.)

Nasheman (Urdu), Ibrahim Saheb Street, Bangalore-560001. (Karnataka)

Noor, 22-8-361/16, Darul Shifa, Hyderabad-500024. (A.P.)

North Eastern Messenger (English) Shillong-793001. (Meghalaya)

Paigam (Daily) (Bengali) 26/1 Market Street, Calcutta-700017. (W.B.)

Pan Islamic, Islamic Library, Near Khiyaban, Sholapur-413001, (Maharashtra).

Prabodhanam Weekly (Malayalam), Silver Hills, Marikunnu, Calicut-673012. (Kerala)

Quadafi, 4-B, MGB Lane, 1st Floor, P.S. Ebalpur, Calcutta-700023. (W.B.)

Radiance, 2448, Baradari Sher Afghan, Ballimaran, Delhi-110006.

Rafeeq-e-Manzil (Urdu) 230, Abul Fazal Enclave, Okhla, New Delhi-110025.

Rahnuma-e-Deccan (Urdu) 5-3-831, Shanker Bagh, Hyderabad-500012. (A.P.)

Ar-Risala, Islamic Centre, Nizamuddin West, New Delhi-110013.

S.I.M. News Bulletin, 4 Abdul Qadir Bldg., Jail Road, Aligarh-202001. (U.P.)

Sadar Huq (Hindi) Plot No. 9, Meerji Colony, M.I. Road, Jaipur-302001. (Rajasthan)

Salav Weekly (Urdu), 103, St. John's Church Road, Bangalore-560005. (Karnataka)

Samarasam (Tamil) (Fortnightly), 78, Perambur High Road, (First Floor) Madras-600012. (T.N.)

Shaheen (Gujarati) Kalupur, Tower, Ahmedabad-380001. (Gujarat)

Shalimar News, Sangareddy P.O., 502001. (A.P.)

Shadab (Urdu), 11-5-147, Red Hills, Hyderabad-560004. (A.P.)

Shantimarg (Marathi), Islami Sahitya Prakashan, Meeraj-416410. (Maharashtra)

Siyasat (Urdu) Jawaharlal Nehru Road, Hyderabad-500001. (A.P.)

Siyasat Jadeed (Daily) (Urdu), Chamanganj, P.B. 418, Kanpur-208001. (U.P.)

Sunmarga (Kannada) (Weekly), Bethi Habi Road, Mangalore-575001. (Karnataka)

Tasneem (Assamese) Ambari Lane, Goalpara-783101. Assam

Al-Taueeyah (Urdu), Islamic Research Academy, 4 Joga Bai, New Delhi-110025.

Uloom-ul-Quran (Urdu), Idara Uloom-ul-*Quran*, Sir Syed Nagar, P.B. 99, Aligarh-202001. (U.P.)

Urdu Times (Urdu) (Daily), 243 Maulana Azad Road, Bombay-400008. (Maharashtra)

Urooj-e-Hind (Urdu) Bangalore-560001. (Karnataka)

Voice of Islam, Calicut-673001. (Kerala)

Young Muslim Digest, Darul Suroor, 43, Dickinson Road, Bangalore-560042. (Karnataka)

Yuvasarani (Youth's Monthly) (Malayalam), Silver Hills, Calicut-673012. (Kerala)
Zindgi-e-Nau (Urdu) 1525, Suiwalan, New Delhi-110002.

COMPLETED DOCTORAL RESEARCH

Arabic

Abbas, Sayed Ali, *Al-Mutanabbi: His life and works*, Lucknow, 1962.
Abidi, Syed Badrul Hasan, *Development of Scholasticism under the Abbasids with special reference to the Mutazilites*, Lucknow, 1966.
Ahmad Ejaz, *The Arabic Poets of India*, Lucknow, 1958.
Ahmad, S. *Ehtisham, Development of Arabic Literary Criticism up to 12th century A.D.* Aligarh, 1967.
Ahmed, Syed Bashir, *Critical Study of Sayyed Qutb as a Modern Writer in the Light of his works and Literary Achievements*, Central Institute of English & Foreign Languages, 1987.
Ahmad, Sayed Iqbal, *Arabic Lexicographers of India*, Lucknow, 1963.
Ahmad, Syed Tufail, *Jafar Mutawakkil al-Allah and his Reign*, Allahabad, 1966.
Alavy, Syed Mohd. Yusuf, *Al Mansur*, Lucknow, 1958.
Ali, Amjad, Kuthaiyir (Ibn-Abdirrahman) Azzah, *An Erotic poet of the Ummayyid period*, Allahabad, 1956.
Arzoo, Mukhtaruddin Ahmed, *A Critical Edition of Al Hamasat al-Basriyya with Notes and Introduction*, Aligarh, 1952.
Avobi, N.A., *The History of the Wahabi Movement from the earliest time up to the present day*, Lucknow, 1956.
Azmi, Moinuddin, *The Contribution of Hameeduddin al-Farrahi to the Interpretation of Quran*, Aligarh, 1970.
Fazlur Rehman, M., *A Critical Edition of Sabhar-al marjan Fiatar-i-Hindustan by Mir Ghulam Ali Azad*, Aligarh, 1961.
Ghayasuddin, *A Critical Analysis of the writings of Abu al-Rehan Mohd. Ibn Ahmad al-Biruni pertaining to India*, Aligarh, 1970.
Hasan, Mujataba, *Arabic Words in Urdu*, Aligarh, 1949.
Huq, *Mahmudul Mufti Mohammad Abdulu: His Life and Works*, Aligarh, 1964.

Jafri, Syed Husain Mohammad, *The Concept of God in Islam with special reference to the Nahjal Balagha: A Comparative study*, Lucknow, 1960.

Khan, Hamid Ali, *Arabic Poetry in India, Aligarh,* 1963.

Kutty, Ahmad, *Life of Prophet Muhammed as depicted in his Contemporary Poetry*, University of Calicut, 1980.

Mustafa, H. Ghulam, *Religious Trends in Pre-Islamic Arabic Poetry*, Aligarh, 1962.

Naqvi, M.R., *Alkhwarij*, Lucknow.

Sadia, Haleema, *Arab wa Hind ke Talluqat*, Nagpur, 1987.

Siddiqui, Mohd. Siddique, *Walid iba Abdil Malik*, Allahabad, 1959.

Tirmidhi, Baqirali Mohammadali, *The Contribution of the Muslims of Gujarat to Arabic Language and Literature*, Bombay, 1947.

Economics

Guha, A., *Economic Transition of Afghanistan, 1929-61*, I.S.I.S., Delhi, 1963.

Khan, M. Mazhar, *Trade and Industries of India from 1700 to 1750 from English, Persian and Indigenous Sources* (Hindi & Urdu), Allahabad, 1966.

Kulshreshtha, S.S., *Development of Trade and Industry under the Mughals 1526 A.D. to 1707 A.D.* Rajasthan, 1955.

Narayan, B.K., *Economic Development of Hyderabad State*, Mysore, 1959.

Seth, K.L., *Pattern of Economic Development in Pakistan*, I.S.I.S., Delhi, 1967.

Siddiqi, Noman Ahmad, *Land Revenue Administration under the Mughals in the first half of the 18th century*, Aligarh, 1960.

Tahtooh, H. Ali, *Commercial Relations between the Arab World and India (9th to 10th centuries)*, University of St. Andrews, U.K., 1986.

Yusufuddin, M., *Economic Theories of Islam*, Osmania, 1947.

Education

Bassam, Abdul Razak Al-Hasso, *English for Specific Purposes: Techniques and Problems with Specific Reference to the Teaching of English to Medical Students of Salahudeen University, Iraq,* J.N.U., 1989.

Chowdhury, G. Subhani, *Entry to Higher Education in Bangladesh: An Investigation into Students Characteristics,* Baroda, 1987.

Faroqui, S.S.M. Mazheruddin, *Study of Alienation of Muslim Minority students in Telengana area in relation to their Educational and other Demographic Factors,* Osmania, 1988.

Fuster, Joachim, *Comparative Analysis of the Relationship between acceptance of self and acceptance of others in four Indian college student communities – Hindu, Muslim, Catholics and Zorostrian,* Baroda, 1959.

Ghulam Rasool, M., *Educational aspect of the thought of Maulana Azad: Being an analysis of ideas of Maulana Azad on Educational problems,* Delhi, 1970.

Hasan, Anwarul, *The message of Islamic Education in the Medieval Period,* Lucknow, 1958.

Jain, M.A., *Aligarh Movement: Its origin and development, 1857-1906,* Agra, 1962.

Khan, M. Hussain, *Education in the Tamil Country from 1700 to 1857 A.D.* Madras, 1988.

Lelyveld, D.S., *Aligarh's first generation Muslim solidarity and English education in Northern India, 1857–1900,* Chicago, 1975.

Pathan, N.M., *Critical study of the causes responsible for the educational backwardness of the Muslim women and to suggest ways and means for improvement,* Shivaji, 1986.

Phirozuddin, *Sayyid Shah Waliullah's Philosophy of Education,* Bombay, 1952.

Quraishi, M.A., *Muslim Education and Learning in Gujarat,* 1297–1758 A.D. Baroda, 1960.

Rehman, A.A., *Muslim Educational system in Iraq during the Abbasid period,* Aligarh, 1964.

Suhay, B.K., *North Indian education and learning under the great Mughals (1526–1707 A.D.)* Ranchi, 1965.

Shahrban, P.A., *Potentiality of certain elements of traditional culture among Muslims in Kerala for multi-dimensional models of non-formal education,* Kerala, 1987.

Sharma, K.D., *Equalisation and utilisation of educational opportunities with reference to Muslim community in Delhi,* Jamia, 1975.

Siddiqui, Shahjahan, *Standardisation of a test in creative thinking for Urdu speaking student at formal operative state in Telengana area, A.P. State*, Osmania, 1988.

History

Abrol, Prem Kumar, *Role of the nobility under Babar and Humayun*, Allahabad, 1965.

Ahmad, Ali, *Inter-regional linkages in north-west India during early* Mughals, J.N.U., 1988.

Ahmad, Mohammad Taqi, *Nasiruddin Hyder, King of Oudh*, Lucknow, 1954.

Ahmed, Q., *Wahabee Movement in Bihar*, Patna 1962.

Ahmad, Safi, *Two kings of Awadh: Mohammed Ali Shah and Amjad Ali Shah 1837–1847*, Lucknow, 1966.

Ahmad, S. Wasi, *Hajjaj-ibn-Yusuf*, Bihar, 1962.

Alvi, Mohammad Rizwan, *The Capital cities of the Muslim Capliphate: A literary, architectural, social and economic account of Daruasous, Baghdad and Cordova*, Lucknow, 1957.

Ansari, Jabir Ali, *Hazrat Umar Farookh kee Uplabdhiyan, Rohilkhand* (K.G.K. College, Moradabad), 1988.

Ansari, Mohammad Iqbal, *The Arab League: Its establishment and role in the Arab world*, Aligarh, 1963.

Awasthi, Dhyaneshwar, *Sir Spencer Harcourt Butler's administration in the United Provinces of Agra and Oudh, 1918–1922*, Banaras, 1963.

Basu, Kamalkrishna, *The Adil Sahis of Bijapur*, Calcutta, 1940.

Banerjee, Jamini Mohan, *History of Firoz Shah Tughluq*, Allahabad, 1959.

Bhargava, Visheshwar Sarup, *Marwar and Mughal emperors 1526 A.D. to 1748 A.D.*, Rajasthan, 1963.

Bhatnagar, G.D., *Administration of Oudh under Wajid Ali Shah*, Lucknow, 1955.

Bhatnagar, S., *Uttar Mughal Kaleen Wazir, 1707–1761*, Banaras Hindu University, 1988.

Bhattacharyya, Sudhindranath, *Mughal relations with the north-eastern frontier states of Cooch Behar, Kamrup and Assam, Calcutta*, 1934.

Blake, S.P., *Darul Khilfat-i, Shahjahanabad: The Padsharni Shahar in Mughal India, 1556–1739*, Chicago, 1974.

Chand, T.P., *The Administration of Oudh, 1858 A.D. to 1877 A.D.* Gorakhpur, 1967.

Chatterji, N.L., *Mir Qasim's rule in Bengal,* Lucknow, 1934.

Chaturvedi, Kailash Chandra. *The Annexation of Awadh.* Agra, 1960.

Chauba, Jharkhande, *History of the Gujarat Kingdom 1458–1537,* Banaras, 1967.

Choudhary, H., *Consensus and Political development perspectives in the History of Bangladesh, 1947–72,* Calcutta, 1988.

Chaudhuri, Ira, *The Nizam Shahi Kingdom of Ahmadnagar 1490–1600 A.D. with special reference to Chand Sultana,* Calcutta, 1967.

Chaudhuri, N.G., *British relations with Hyderabad, 1798–1843.* Calcutta, 1961.

Choudhry, S.R., *Al Hajjaj ibn Yusuf: An examination of his works and personality,* Delhi, 1960.

Das, Ranajitkumar, *Career of Prince Shah Shuja,* Calcutta, 1970.

Desai, Shantilal Keshavlal, *Lives and times of Mahmud Shah I and Muzaffar Shah II of Gujarat,* Baroda, 1966.

Devapriam, E., *Influence of Western art on Mughal Painting,* Case Western Reserve, 1972.

Dwivedi, S.D., *The Relations of Rajputs with Delhi Sultans,* Gorakhpur, 1968.

Eswari, Kama Shankar. *The War of Independence in Awadh 1857–1858,* Agra, 1960.

Hallissey, R.C., *Rajput Rebellion against Aurangzeb: A study in Rajput, Mughal relations,* Missouri, Columbia, 1973.

Haqqi, S. Anwarul Haque, *Chinghiz Kha,* Aligarh, 1954.

Hohsainpur, Rahman, *Hindu-Muslim relations in Bengal, 1905–1947,* Calcutta, 1968.

Jawhari, Ramesh Chandra, *Firoz Tughluq,* Agra, 1965.

Kunango, Kalikaranjan, *Main thesis:* (1) *Sher Shah:* (2) *History of the Jats and Dara Shikoh, Subsidiary Thesis:* (1) *Prince Mohammad Dara Shikoh and Mirza Rajah Jai Singh Kuchhwah: Some correspondence between Prince Shah Shuja and the Emperor Shah Jahan;* and *Some sidelights on the Character and Court life of Shah Jahan,* Calcutta, 1930.

Kareem, C.K.A., *Kerala under Hyder Ali and Tipu Sultan,* Aligarh, 1970.

Lal, Kishori Saran, *Alauddin Muhammad Khilji,* Allahabad, 1945.

Malik, Zahiruddin, *Muhammad Shah, 1719–1748,* Aligarh, 1960.

Mandal, Susila, *Expansion of Muslim Powers in Bengal 1200 A.D. to 1526 A.D.* Calcutta, 1961.

Mathur, Mitthan Lal, *Mewar in Pre-Mughal India*, Rajasthan, 1955.

Mehra, Shrikrishna Das. *The Life and Times of Amir Khan 1768–1834*, Vikram, 1966.

Mehta, Sumant Goverdhanraj, *Persian Sources of the History of Muslim India contributed by Hindus*, Gujarat, 1960.

Mukherjee, Ansuman, *History of Oudh 1801–1856*, Patna, 1963.

Nigam, K.C., *Ghaziuddin Hyder, First King of Oudh*, Lucknow, 1947.

Pandey, Avadh Behari, *History of First Afghan Empire in India*, Allahabad, 1949.

Parmu, R.K., *History of Kashmir from Shahmir to Shah Jahan*, Allahabad, 1948.

Qidwai, Mushtaq Karim, *Commercial and Cultural Relations between India and Arabia*, Lucknow, 1962.

Rahman, M.A., *Critical Analysis of the Nizam's Government's Policies regarding Social and Political Problems in the state, 1935–48*, Osmania, 1987.

Rastogi, R.S., *Indo-Afghan Relations, 1881–1900*, Lucknow, 1957.

Ray, Sukumar, *Humayun in Persia*, Calcutta, 1959.

Regani, Sarojini, *Nizam-British Relations, 1724–1857*, Osmania, 1960.

Rizvi, S.A.A., *Abul Fazal and his Times*, Agra, 1949.

Sahgal, Shiva Pyari, *Economic and Social Life in India in the first half 17th Century*, Allahabad, 1964.

Samadi, S.B., *Mamun, the Abbasia: His Life and History*, Lucknow, 1943.

Sarkar, Jagadisnarayan, *The life of Mir Jumla, the General of Aurangzeb*, Calcutta, 1948.

Sen, Anjali, *Life and Work of Murshid Quli Khan*, Calcutta.

Sharma, G.N., *Mewar and Mughal Emperors 1526–1707*, Agra, 1951.

Sheik Ali, B., *Foreign Policy of Tipu Sultan*, Aligarh, 1956.

Shukla, Santosh Kumar, *A History of the Bangash Nawabs of Farrukhabad 1813–1858*, Agra, 1965.

Shyam, Radhey, *Rise and Fall of the Kingdom of Ahmadnagar*, Allahabad, 1958.

Siddiqi, M. Zamiruddin, *Muslim Religious Movements in India in the 18th century*, Aligarh, 1966.

Singh, Ganda, *Ahmad Shah Durrani*, Panjab, 1952.

Sinha, Parmeshwar Prasad, *Biography of Raja Birbal*, Bhagalpur, 1969.
Singh, R.K.B., *Life of Badruddin Tayabji and His Role in the National Movement*, Magadh, 1989.
Sinha, Surendra Nath, *History of the Subah of Allahabad under the Mughals 1526 A.D. to 1707 A.D.* Allahabad, 1963.
Srivastava, A.B.L., *History of Shujauddaula*, Agra, 1938.
Srivastav, Ashirbadi Lal, *First two Nawabs of Oudh*, Lucknow, 1932.
Srivastav, Pandey Harish Chandra, *History of Uttar Pradesh during the Sultanate 1206 A.D. to 1526 A.D.* Gorakhpur, 1970.
Thakur, Upendra, *Studies in Political and Cultural History of Mithila from the earliest times to the Mughal conquest*, Calcutta, 1954.
Tripathi, G.P., *Indo-Afghan Relations 1882–1907*, Delhi, 1907.
Varma, Bhagwat Dayal. *Muslim Epigraphy in S.W. India with special reference to Kolhapur, Panhala, Janjira, Raibag, Miraj, Bijapur, Ahmedabad, Rahanatpur etc.*, Bombay, 1965.
Verma, Dinesh Chandra, *Some Aspects of the History of Bijapur*, Lucknow, 1966.
Verma, Virendra, *Najibuddaulah: His Life and Times*, Aligarh.

Law

Diwan, Paras Nath, *Parental Control and Jural Concepts of Guardianship and Custody – Their Origin and development in modern law: Comparative study under Roman law, Hindu Law, Mohammedan Law and English Law*, Punjab, 1967.
Jain, Baldev Singh, *Administration of Justice in the 17th century India*, Agra, 1968.
Multalib, M.A., *Administration of Justice under the Nizam, 1724–1947*, Osmania, 1958.
Razi, Hanifa, *Abdullah Ibn Masood and His Legal System*, Aligarh, 1967.
Sangam, Satya Prakash, *Crime and Punishment in Mughal India*, Poona, 1957.
Suhrawardy, A.M., *Sources of Muslim Law*, Calcutta, 1908.

Persian

Abbasi, Mohd. Motasim, *A Critical Study of Persian Literature during Khilji period 1290–1320*, Aligarh, 1968.

Ali, Shaikh Mohammed Yusuf Raza, *The Persian Literature under Jahangir and Shahjahan*, Bombay, 1954.

Ahmad, Saeed, *Survey of Persian Literature in Afghanistan*, Aligarh, 1946.

Ahmad, Syed Maqbool, *Edition and Annotation of a manuscript in Persian: Majmuai Danish, a collection of letters and petitions from the Nawabs of Broach to the Emperor Shah Alam and Vazirs etc.*, written by Keshwar Das, son of Chhabili Das Desai (period extending approximately from 1758 to 1788). Allahabad, 1959.

Alavi, Mohd. Rizvan, *The Development of Persian Language and Literature under the Patronage of Lodhi Sultan of Delhi*, Lucknow, 1961.

Ansari, Noor-ul-Hasan, *Indo-Persian Literature during the latter half of the 17th century A.D.* Delhi, 1964.

Ashraf, S. Waheed, *A Critical Edition of the Lataif-i-Ashrafi*, Aligarh, 1966.

Barlaskar, D. Hussain, *Influence of Persian on Assamese*, Gauhati University, 1985.

Batliwala, Sorab Hirjibhoy, *Evolution of the Modern Persian Language: Being a philological dissertation on its history, grammar and rhetoric*, Bombay, 1964.

Bilgrami, Rafat Fatima. *Religious and Quasi-religious departments of the Mughals 1556–1707*, Aligarh, 1968.

Devare, Tukaram Nagesh. *A Short History of Persian Literature at the Bahmani, the Adilshahi and Qutabshahi Courts*, Bombay, 1945.

Durani, Dawarika Nath, *The Contribution of Kashmiri writers to Indo-Persian Literature from 1556 A.D. to 1650 A.D.*, Delhi 1969.

Fakhruzzaman, Ummi Hani, *Account of Persian Poets connected with India as contained in Nafaisul Maasir*, Aligarh, 1958.

——, *A Critical Edition of the Nafaisul Maasir with a critical Introduction*, Lucknow, 1965.

Gai, Bahadur Manekji, *Life and Pre-Islamic Iran as gleaned from Persian Masnavis*, Bombay, 1948.

Gorekar, Nizamuddin Sharafuddin, *Influence on Persian of Indian Life and Letters*, Bombay, 1966.

Hasrat, Bikramjit, *An Introduction to the Works of Dara Shikoh*, Calcutta, 1944.

Hassanullah, Syed, *Hindu's Contribution to Persian in the Eighteenth century India*, Gauhati, 1985.

Husain, Ragheeb, *Development of Persian Masnavi*, Allahabad, 1955.

Imamuddin, S.M., *The Critical edition of the Tarikh-i-Khan-i-Jahani of Wa Makhzan-i-Afgani of Nimat Allah with Introduction and summary of the Tarikh*, Calcutta, 1951.

Iqbal, Zohra, *Ghazali: His Life and Works*, Aligarh, 1958.

Khan, Abdul Subhan, *Critical edition of Yusuf Ali Khan's Tarikh-e-Mahabatjang (or Ahwal-e-Aliverdi Khan)* with English translation and introduction, Calcutta, 1965.

Khan, Anwar Ali, *Religious Ideas of Jamaluddin at Afghani*, Aligarh, 1963.

Khan, Yusuf Ali, *Critical edition of Maasir-e-Asafi: A History of the Nizams of the Deccan by Lachminarayan Shafiq*. Osmania, 1966.

Kirmani, H.A. *Persian Literature during the period of Jahangir*, Banaras Hindu University, 1979.

Mannan, Mohd. Abdul, *Persian Literature under the Bahmani Regime*, Osmania, 1966.

Miran, Shaikh Muhammed, *Contribution of Gujarat to Persian Literature during 1400 A.D. and 1900 A.D.*, Bombay, 1968.

Naik, Chhotubhai Ranchhodji, *Abdur Rahim Khan Khanan and his Literary Circle*, Bombay, 1942.

Pal, Harendra Chandra, *Jalaluddin Rumi and his Tasawuf*, Calcutta, 1960.

Quraishi, A.N. *Persian Poetry under the later Mughal period*, Gujarat, 1969.

Qureshi, Shamim Ahmad, *Indian Stories in Persian Literature*, Delhi, 1968.

Rahman, Mojibur, *Important Allusions and References in Persian Poetry*, Bihar, 1970.

Rasheed, Ghulam Dastagir, *The Development of Natia Poetry in Persian Literature*, Osmania, 1957.

Rizvi, S.A.M., *Mirza Ghazi Beg Terkhan and his Patronage of Art and Letters*, Lucknow, 1957.

Rizvi, S.M. Fida Abbas. *A Critical study of the Tazkiras of Persian Poets compiled in India from the middle of the 16th to the middle of the 17th century A.D.*, Aligarh, 1962.

Sadrangani, Harumal Isardas, *The Persian Poets of Sindh: A critical study dealing with the thought and work of the Representative Persian poets of Sindh through the ages*, Bombay, 1946.

Saxena, Ram Kishore, *Edward Fitzzerald: Influence of Persian thought on his verse*, Agra, 1964.

Siddiqui, N.J., *Critical editing of Diwan-i-Sirajuddin Ali Khan Arzu*, Delhi, 1987.

Philosophy

Abadani, Farshad Sham, *The Early rise of Mysticism in Iran*, Bombay, 1953–56.

Ahmad, Qazi Moinuddin, *History of the Shattari Silsilah*, Aligarh, 1964.

Akhtar, S. Waheed, *Khaja Mir Dard's Contribution to Sufism*, Osmania, 1961.

Ansari, M.A.H., *Ethical Philosophy of Miskawaih: An Exposition and Critical Examination*, Aligarh, 1961.

Batra, Sriniwas, *Hindi and Persian Sufi Poetry: A Comparative Study*, Punjab, 1967.

Bhatnagar, R.S., *Philosophy of Sufism in Urdu Poetry with special reference to Mir Taqi Dard, Atish and Ghalib*, Allahabad, 1960.

Eaton, R.M., *Sufis of Bijapur, 1300–1700 Social Rolls of Sufis in Medieval India*, University of Wisconsin.

Ghazi, Abdullah, *Raja Rammohan Roy (1772–1883): Encounter with Islam and Christianity. The Articulation of Hindu Self-consciousness*, Harvard, 1975.

Goven, Rafik, *Absolution of Sankaracharya as compared with Maulana Rumi's School of Thought*, Banaras, 1958.

Gupta, B.P., *Self in Spinoza and Ibn-ul-Arabi*, Allahabad, 1954.

Hanif Mohd. *Naqshbandia, Mujaddidiya, Mazharia System of Sufism*, Agra, 1964.

Haq, Mohammad Enamul. *A History of Sufism in Bengal*, Culcutta, 1934.

Hussain, regheeb, *Sufism in India*, Bihar. 1964.

Khatoon, Jamila. *Place of God, Man and Universe in the Philosophical System of Iqbal*, Aligarh, 1962.

Khundmiri, S. Alam, *Iqbal's Concept of Time: Its Relation to Contemporary Western thought*, Osmania, 1969.

Nasira, A.M., *Naqshbandi System of Sufism (Mysticism)*, Osmania, 1957.

Noor Nabi, M., *Develop of Muslim Religious thought in India from 1200 A.D. to 1450 A.D.*, Aligarh, 1958.

Rafeeque, M., *Comparative Study of the Philosophy of Sri Aurobindo and Dr. Iqbal*, Aligarh, 1969.

Shaikh, Zuleikha, *Mysticism of Jalaluddin Rumi*, Karnataka, 1969.

Siddiqi, M. Murtuza, *Qadriyya System of Sufism*, Osmania, 1960

Siddiqi, Zafar A., *Philosophy of Ibn Tufayl*, Aligarh, 1948.

Siddiqui M. Safiuddin, *At Ghazali and Islamic Mysticism: A Critical and Historical Sketch*, Marathwada, 1968.

Siddiqui, M. Suleiman, *Sufis of the Deccan: 1347-1538 A.D.* Osmania, 1975.

Tirnizi, B.A., *Muslim Saints of Ahmedabad and Patna*, Gujarat, 1967.

Political Science

Abidi, M.A.H.H., *Jordan 1948–57: A Political study with Special Reference to the Problem of Integration of the Palestinian and Trans-Jordanian Arabs*, Delhi, 1962.

Agarwal, V.K., *Indo-Bangladesh Relations, 1971–1980*, Meerut, 1986.

Ahmad, Ishtiaq, *Anglo-Iranian Relations, 1905–1919*, Aligarh, 1964.

Alam, A.Y. Shamsul, *Muslims and Bengal Politics, 1912–24*, JNU, 1985.

Ali, Abbas, *Role of Jewish in the Arab-Israeli Conflict*, Aligarh, 1976.

Arghandanvi, A. Ali, *British Imperialism and Afghanistan's Struggle for Independence 1904–1933*, JNU, 1976.

Arora, B.D., *Indian-Indonesian Relations, 1961-1967*, JNU, 1974.

Arya, H.C., *Study of some aspects of the Relations of the U.S. with Pakistan, 1947–59*, I.S.I.S., Delhi, 1967.

Bahadur, Kalim, *Jamat-i-Islami of Pakistan: Political thought and Political Action*, JNU, 1976.

Bandyopadhyay, A.K., *Problem of National Integration in Malaya with Special Reference to the Citizenship System between Malayan Union and Mardeka*, Calcutta, 1977.

Barman, Rakta K., *Foreign Policy of Malaya – 31st August, 1975 to 16th September*, 1963, JNU, 1969.

Barnett, R.B., *Regional Policies in a Mughal successor state: Nawab of Awadha, 1720–1785*, California, 1975.

'Becker, M.L., *All India Muslim League, 1906–1974: A Study of Leadership in Evolution of a Nation*, Harvard, 1957.

Beg, Mohd. Ali, *Indonesian Struggle for Independence, 1914–1955*, Aligarh, 1958.

Behera, Basank K., *Confrontation to Cooperation – A study of Malaysian-Indonesian Relations, 1965–1968*, JNU, 1976.

Bilgrami, A.H., *Indo-Afghan Relations in the 19th century 1799–1907*, Aligarh, 1955.

Chakrabarti, Gargi, *Gandhi and the Hindu-Muslim Problems, 1919–1929*, Calcutta, 1977.

Chakrabarty, S.K., *Evolution of Politics in Bangladesh since 1947*, Sambalpur, 1947.

Chandra, Satish, *Parties and Politics in Mughal Court*, Allahabad, 1948.

Chaturvedi, D.K., *Pakistan's Relations with China, 1947–65*, JNU, 1970.

Das, G., *Indo-Iranian Relations since 1878*, Lucknow, 1954.

Das, P.K., *Indo-Pak Relations from 1966 to 1972*, Vikram.

Elgohary, A. Hadi, *Relations between U.S.A. and the Arab World with Special Reference to the Relation with Egypt*. Aligarh, 1970.

Al-Eryani, A. Qawi, *Non-aligned Movement and the Arab World*, Delhi, 1988.

Gani, H.A., *National Integration: Certain Muslim Political Issues*, Marathwada, 1975.

Gautam, Brijendra B., *Rise and Growth of Nationalism in the Middle East, 1920–1950*, Lucknow, 1961.

Ghosh, D.K., *England and Afghanistan: A Phase in their Relations*, Calcutta, 1958.

Ghosh, Shyamali, *Awami League, 1962–71*, JNU, 1973.

Gilmartin, D.P., *Growth of the Muslim League in the Punjab, 1937–1947*, Berkelam, California, 1976.

Goswami, R.B.L., *Critical study of Indo-Pakistan Relations, 1965–72*, Agra.

Graham, Gail Minault, *Khilafat Movement: A Study of Indian Muslim Leadership, 1919–1924*. Pennsylvania, 1972.

Gupta, Raghuraj, *Hindu-Muslim Relations in the city of Dehradun*, Lucknow, 1960.

Gurbux, Gope Ramkrishan, *Oudh under Wellesley: The study of the Political Intercourse between Marques Wellesley and Nawab Saheb Ali Khan of Oudh,* Bombay, 1944.

Haendel, D., *Process of Priority Formulation: U.S. Foreign Policy in the Indo-Pakistan War of 1971*, Pennsylvania, 1976.

Hawadyar M. Omer, *Pakhtunistan issue as an element in Afghan Foreign Policy: A Legacy of Imperialisation*, JNU, 1987.

Husain, Habib, *Development of Political Institutions in the Abbassid Caliphate: 8th century onwards*, Lucknow, 1967.

Iqbal, Sheikh Mohd., *Political Development in Najd and the Hijar 1900–1934*, I.S.I.S. Delhi, 1963.

Jha, D.C., *Indo-Pakistani relations, 1960–65*, I.S.I.S. Delhi, 1973

Jha, R.N., *United States and the Kashmir Problem, 1947–58. The Conflict Analysis and the Attitude of Super Power*, Bhagalpur, 1976.

Jhaveri, Satyavati S., *Presidency in Indonesia: August 1945-March 1957 with Special Reference to a few factors that shaped its Evolution during the period*, Bombay, 1968.

Johari, Jagdish C. *India and Indonesia: A Study in International Relations*, 1945–60, Agra, 1964.

Jrare, Vijaykumar L.R., *Arab-Israel Dispute Since 1948*. Vikram, 1975.

Kaur, S., *Critical Study of Muslim Politics in India from 1858 to 1906 with Special Reference to the Role of Sir Syed Ahmed*, Agra, 1975.

Khaja, Moinuddin, *Study of Muslim Political Ideas in India, 1919–1947*, Marathwada, 1970.

Khan, Abid Raza, *Development of the Nationalism in Egypt, 1870–1914*, Aligarh, 1964.

Khan, Ahtiran Wali, *Freedom Struggle in Faizabad, 1857–1947*, Avadh, 1978.

Khan, Glam Hassan, *Freedom Movement in Kashmir, 1931–1940*, Kashmir, 1978.

Khan, Rasheeduddin A., *Political Development in Iraq, 1914–1932*, Delhi, 1962.

Khwaja, Habibuddin, *India's Relations with the Arab world with Particular Reference to Egypt and U.A.R. 1947–63*, Aligarh, 1970.

Kidwai, M.H., *Islamic State and other Muslim Political Institutions from 7th century to 10th century A.C.*, Lucknow (n.d.).

Kidwai, M. Asif, *Protection of Minorities in India*, Lucknow, 1947.

Kidwai. M. Hashim, *Origin and Development of the Islamic state in the first century A.H.* Aligarh, 1961.

Kishore, Mohd. Ali, *Jan Sangh's Approach to Problems of India's Foreign Policy,* Aligarh, 1968.

Krishnamurthy, S., *Central Local Relations in Indonesia 1947–1959,* Delhi, 1963.

Kukreja, V., *Civil Military Relations in South Asia with Special Reference to Pakistan, Bangladesh and India,* Delhi, 1989.

Kumar, Bharat, *Super Power and the West Asian Crisis of 1967,* JNU 1973.

Lal Bahadur, *All India Muslim League: Its History, Activities and Achievements,* Agra, 1953.

Mandel, B.L., *India's Relations with Malaya and Indonesia, 1793–1833,* Bhagalpur, 1967.

Mani, V.K., *Pakistan's Relations with Iran, 1947–74,* JNU, 1975.

Meyers, A.E., *Theodore Beck and Sajjid Ahmad Khan: The Myth of Proveocateur and Puppet in Muslim Separatism, 1875–1909.* American University, 1973.

Miller, J.M., *India as a factor in Pakistan's Foreign Policy: A study of the Attitudes and Influences of the Political Parties, pess, groups and elites,* Rajasthan, 1967.

Mishra, A.S., *Indo-Pakistani Conflict and British Policy, 1947–1966,* JNU, 1976.

Misra, K.K., *Kashmir as Problem of India's Foreign Policy,* Allahabad, 1963.

Misra, Satish Chandra, *Political History of the Sur Dynasty,* Banaras, 1950.

Al-Mujahid, Sharif, *Indian Secularism: A Case Study of Muslim* Minority, Karachi, 1970.

Mumtaz, Zaimul Abedin, *Afghanistan's Relations with Iran,* Aligarh, 1976.

Mustafa, A.J., Abid, *Arab Bath Socialist Party and the Congress Party: A Contemporary study of Social Basis and Organisational Structure,* Delhi, 1987.

Nagpal, O.P., *Indonesia: An Experiment in Guided Democracy, 1859–1865,* Indore, 1969.

Nizami, Z.A., *Role of the Nationalist Muslims in Indian Politics,* Jawaji, 1973.

Pandher, R. Singh, *Analysis of the Indian Foreign Policy in the Post-Nehru period: A case study of the Bangladesh Crisis Management*, Howard, 1975.

Patil, Hemalata S., *Indira Gandhi and the Bangladesh Issue: A Perspective Study*, Shivaji, 1986.

Printup, R., *Indo-Pakistan Relations: 1962–1967. An events data Approach to Analysing Dyadic International Conflict*, Syracuse, 1976.

Qayyum, S.A., *Egypt's Relations with Great Britain from 1945 to 1954*, Aligarh, 1970.

Quraishi, Z.M., *Wafd party of Egypt: Its Rise and Fall*, Delhi, 1963.

Rehman, M.M., *Non-Alignment with Particular Reference to the Foreign Policies of India and the U.A.R.*, Aligarh, 1969.

Rao, K.V. Narayana, *Emergence of Andhra Pradesh*, Madras, 1967.

Ray, Jayanakumar, *United States-Pakistan: An Alliance, 1953–58*, Jadavpur, 1965.

Raychaudhuri, Makhanlal, *The State and Religion in Mughal India*, Calcutta, 1949.

Rizvi, Syed Athar Abbas, *Muslim Revivalist Movements in Northern India in 16th and 17th centuries*, Agra, 1962.

Sawant, A.B., *Egypt's Sub-Saharan Africa Policy, 1952–70: Objectives, Implementation and Assessment*, JNU, 1976.

Sen, Shila, *Muslim Policies in Bengal, 1937–1947*, JNU, 1976.

Shah, A. Hadi, *Civil War and International Intervention: the 1971 Indo-Pakistan Crisis*, Claremont Graduate School, 1974.

Shankukhnathan, S.K., *Security Council and Kashmir Question: A Study in big Power politics*, Poona, 1970.

Sheran, Anjoo, *Right to Self Determination with Particular Reference to the case of Bangladesh*, BHU, 1982.

Siddiqui, Sham M., *Political Ideas of Sir Syed Ahmed Khan*. Allahabad, 1963.

Singh, M.K., *Political Condition of Bihar on the eve of Muslim rule*, Magadh, 1988.

Singh, S.K., *Role of Bihar's Muslims in Indian National Movement*, Patna, 1975.

Singh, Vishal, *Indonesian Political Parties*, Delhi, 1963.

Sinha, S.C., *Mandates System with Special Preference to Palestine*, Lucknow, 1943.

Sofi, G. Rasool, *Britain's withdrawal from the Persian Gulf*, JNU, 1977.

Sreen, Anuradha, *India and Afghanistan, 1907–1921*, JNU 1975.

Srinivas, M.V., *American View of Muslim Separation in India, 1939–47*, JNU, 1974.

Srivastava, R.K., *India's Relations with Arab East. 1947–1964: Nehru period*, Kanpur, 1977.

Sumati, V. *Modernization of the Nizam's Administration: Socio-Political Linkages in the Nineteenth Century*, Hyderabad, Hyderabad, 1988.

Suryanarayan, V., *Singapore Malaya Relations 1957–65*, I.S.I.S. Delhi, 1969.

Tandon, B.N., *Anglo-Iranian Relations: A Diplomatic study 1878–1900*, Lucknow, 1963.

Taunk, Bengali Mal, *Role of Khilafat Movement in Indian Politics: A Detailed study of the Indian Khilafat Movement of 1919–1924*, Agra, 1963.

Varghese, K.V., *India and Pakistan: A Study in International Relations*, Agra, 1962.

Vyas, Purandar, *Political Institutions of Mughal period and their Ideological Basis*, Vikram, 1979.

Watts, F.T., Jr., *Comparative study of Crises: Selected Periods of Indo-Pakistan Relations*, South Carolina, 1974.

Yanuck, M., *Muslims of the United Provinces 1906–1922: The Politics of a Community*, Chicago, 1973.

Zafri, M.A. Shah, *Indo-Afghan Relations 1947–67*, Punjab, 1972.

Zaman, M., *Afghanistan and the United Nations*, JNU, 1972

Sociology

Ahmad, S. Nesar, *Hindu-Muslim Conflict in India: A World System Perspective*, State University of New York at Binghamton, 1987.

Ali, M.I.A. Ñisar, *Social Relations among the Assamese Muslims in Rural and Urban Situation*, Gauhati, 1975.

Ali, Mohammad Athar, *The Mughal Nobility under Aurangzeb*, Aligarh. 1964.

Asiri, Fazl Mahammud, *Shah Wali Allah and his Hujjatullahil Baligha*, Calcutta, 1952.

Begum, S.R., *Quantitative study of Dermatoglyphic Features among the Hindus and Muslims of Assam*, Dibrugarh, 1973.

Chanderprabha, *Nobility under Akbar, 1556–1605 A.D.*, BHU, 1988.

Cherian, Amprayil, *The Impact of Islam on South India*, Bombay. 1961.

Chopra, Pran Nath, *Some Aspects of Society and Culture during the Mughal age 1526–1707 based mainly on foreign travellers*, Punjab, 1951.

D'Souza, Victor S., *Shaffi Muslims of the east coast of India: A social Survey*, Karnataka, 1952–55.

Durre-e-Shahwar, *Arab women through the Ages: A Socio-cultural study of Arab women in the Pre-Islamic and Post-Islamic period*, Lucknow, 1958.

Farjad, M. Husain, *Comparative Sociological study of student's Behaviour in Aligarh Muslim University and Tehran University*, Aligarh, 1973.

Faroqi, Munir A., *Cooperation, Competition and Group Structure*, Madras, 1962.

Fatima, Parveen, *Awadh ke Nawabon kee Sanskriti: Lucknow per Adharit ek Samajik Itihasik Adhyayan* (in Hindi), BHU, 1988.

Fatma, Nikhat, *Attitude of Muslim women of Aligarh Muslim University – Relations and Adjustments*, Aligarh, 1975.

Fuster, Joachim, *Comparative Analysis of the Relationship between Acceptance of Self and Acceptance of others in Four Indian college student communities – Hindu, Muslim, Catholic and Zorostrian*, Baroda, 1959.

Ghosh, Sulaiman Abu, *A Socio-psychological study of Modern Kuwait*, Delhi, 1970.

Gupta, R., *Hindu-Muslim Relations in the city of Dehradun*, Lucknow, 1960.

Haider, S.H., *Manners and Customs of the Muslims in the United Province*, Bombay, 1941.

Hilal, A. Alim, *Social Philosophy of Dr. Mohammed Iqbal: A Critical Study*, Bhagalpur, 1974.

Hussain, Maqitual., *In Search of an Identity – Muslims in Contemporary India: A Sociological Analysis*. Rutgers, 1982.

Husain, S. Abrar, *Marriage Customs of the Shia Muslims in U.P.: Based on a study of the Marriage Customs of the Shias of Major cities of Uttar Pradesh*, Lucknow, 1967.

Indukumari, M., *Education and Social status of Muslims Women in Kerala*, Kerala, 1976.

Jain, Som Prakash, *Social Structure of Hindu Muslim Community in Uttar Pradesh*, Punjab, 1961–68.

Khan, Nasir Ali, *Changing Pattern of Marriage in Uttar Pradesh: A Psycho-social study of Marriages under the special marriage act 1954 during the first three and a half years. January 1955 to June 1958: Its administration in the State*, Lucknow, 1963.

Khan, Nazir, M.G., *Socio-Economic Survey of the Muslims of Poona*, Bombay, 1946–52.

Kutty, T.M.A., *Rahman, Marriage and Kinship in an Island Society*, Sangar, 1965.

Mekhani, Ghulam M., *Social Background of Hindu Muslim Relationship*, Bombay, 1938–47.

Metcalf, Barbara, *Reformist Ulama: Muslim Religious Leadership in India, 1860–1900*, California, 1975.

Miller, R.E. *Mappila Muslims of Southwest India – A study in Islamic Trends*, Hartford Seminary, 1973.

Misra, Rekha, *Position of Women in Mughal period in Northern India 1526–1748*, Allahabad, 1965.

Mokhapati, J., *Analytical study on fertility and family Planning Practices among Muslims and Christians in Visakhpatnam*, Andhra, 1979.

Nandanikar, S.B., *Muslim Divorced women in Kolhapur District*, Shivaji, 1988.

Nasser, B., *Investigation into the Causes of Indiscipline in Secondary Schools of Iran with Special Reference to Tehran*, Bombay, 1973.

Nigam, Shiva Bindeshawari Prasad, *Nobility under the Sultans of Delhi from 1206 A.D. to 1398 A.D.*, Agra, 1965.

Roy, Shibani, *Status of Muslim women in North India – A Study in the Dynamics of Change*, Delhi, 1976.

Saikia, Mohinik, *Early Assam Muslim Relations and its Cultural Significance*, Gauhati, 1968.

Seth, Satish C., *Growth of Communalism in India and the Problem of Hindu Muslim relations*, Agra, 1959.

Sethi, R.M., *Attitude of Educational working women about the Position of women in modernizing Societies of India and Turkey: A case study of Chandigarh and Ankara*, Punjab, 1972.

Shabbir, Shaikh, *Muslims of Berar and Family Planning*, Nagpur, 1974.

Sharma, K.D., *Equalization and Utilization of Educational Opportunities with reference to Muslim community in Delhi*, Jamia, 1975.

Sharma, Gopi Nath, *Social Life in Medieval Rajasthan 1500 A.D. to 1800 A.D. with Special reference to Impact of Mughal Influences*, Agra, 1967.

Sharma, Shyam Lal, *Marriage and Family in Neo community: A study in the Synthesis of Hindu and Muslim Cultures*, Agra 1960-67.

Shujaat, Fatima, *Social thought of Hali, Osmania*, 1958.

Siddiqi, M. Muslehuddin, *Social thought of Sir Syed Ahmed Khan*, Osmania, 1961.

Siddiqi, Mohammad Yasin, *Muslim Community and the Orthodox Reaction in Islam*, Lucknow, 1955.

Singh, V.J., *Socio-cultural Factors in Population growth (a sociological study of the factors of population growth of Hindus and Muslims) in rural areas of Barabanki*, Lucknow, 1971.

Srivastava, A.C., *Inter-population Variation among Muslims – A study of genetical Characteristics of Sayyad and Pattern of Lucknow*, Lucknow, 1972.

Umar, M., *Muslim Society in the Northern India in the 18th century*, Aligarh, 1960.

Upadhyaya, Bimal Kumar, *Safeguards of the Scheduled Castes, Scheduled Tribes and Minorities in the Indian constitution and their working*, Sangore, 1965.

Verma, Swarnalata, *Hindu Rajahs in Mughal Aristocracy*, Vikram, 1969.

Urdu

Abbas, Syed Musaiyad, *Principles of Modern Urdu Literary Criticism*, Lucknow, 1966.

Abidi, Syed Zille Hasnain, *Urdu Poetry between Two World Wars*, Allabahad, 1958.

Ahmad, Manzoor, *Maulana Abul Kalam Azad kee adabi Khidmaat*, Gorakhpur, 1967.

Ajmali, Syed Mohammad Ajmal, *Common People's Life in Urdu Fiction*, Allahabad, 1964.

Akhtar, Nures Sayeed, *Mulla Wajhi aur unki Taj-ul-Haqiaqui*, Bombay 1969.

Ali, Hasan Meer Syed Shah, *Biography in Urdu*, Lucknow, 1955.

Ali, Mohammad Chirag, *The development of Urdu Marsiya (Elegy) in Bijapur and Golconda up to 17th century A.D.*, Osmania, 1966.

Anjum, Zakia, *Impact of Socio-economic Conditions on Urdu Literature between the Two World Wars, 1914–1939*, Delhi, 1968.

Azmi, K.R., *Progressive Literary Movement in Urdu*, Aligarh, 1958.

Ashrafi, Abdul Wahab, *The Contribution of Shad Azimabadi to the Development of Urdu prose*, Bihar, 1967.

Askari, Alia Bano, *Contribution of Urdu Poetry to the Struggle for Freedom 1857–1921*, Lucknow, 1963.

Aslam, Mohd., *Bahadur Shah Zafar and his Poetry*, Delhi, 1966.

Azar, Hamidulla Khan, *Urdu shairi aur tasawuf*, Nagpur, 1967.

Azmi, I.M., *Urdu Adab Ke irtiga mein adbi tehreekon ka hissa*, Jammu, 1983.

Baig, Mirza Safdar Ali, *The Influence of Sufism on Urdu Poetry*, Osmania, 1966.

Bedi, Kala Singh, *The Linguistic Relationship between Urdu and Punjabi*, Delhi, 1960.

Begum, Atharunisa, *Ahe-e-Asafjahi mein Urdu Natia Shairi*, Gulbarga, 1987.

Begum, F. Jahen Ara, *Elements of Human Psychology in Urdu short stories*, Bihar, 1983.

Begum, Habeebunisa, *Development of Urdu in Mysore*, Delhi, 1959.

Bilgrami, Hamid Hasan, *Nature Poetry in Urdu*, Allahabad, 1944.

Dalvi, Abdussattar Mohd. Ismail, *Bombay Urdu: A study in Linguistic Behaviour*, Bombay, 1965.

Dalvi, Maimoona Khatoon Abdussattar, *Bombay Shahar mein Urdu, 1914 Tak*, Bombay, 1961.

Elahi, Mohd., *A Critical Survey of Urdu Qasida Nigari*, Aligarh, 1958.

Fakruddin, M.G., *Concept of Women in Urdu Literature*, Tirupati, 1984.

Farooqi, Ehteshamuddin, *Political Consciousness in Urdu Poetry 1857 to 1947*, Vikram, 1967.

Faruqi, Khwaja Ahmad, *Letters and Letter writers in Urdu*, Delhi, 1953.

Farooqui, Mohammad Abdul Hamid, *Editing Amin Gujarati's masnavi Yusuf and Zulekha (Zalaikhan) with Introduction and notes*, Bombay, 1948.

Faruqi, Zakir Husain, *The School of Dabeer in Urdu, Marsiya: Dabistan-e-Dabeer*, Bombay, 1963.

Habibunnisa, *Maharaj Sir Kishan Prashad and his Services to Urdu Literature*, Osmania, 1966.

Hamidi, H.U., *The Development of Modern Urdu nazm and European Influences*, Jammu & Kashmir, 1966.

Hasan, Mehrunnisa, *Contribution of Urdu towards the Attainment of Freedom*, Allahabad, 1956.

Hassan, S.A., *Studies in Sufi erotic poetry*, Bihar, 1961.

Hasan, Syed Rasheedul, *A Comparative study of Urdu and Brajbhasha Grammar*, Osmania, 1968.

Hasan, Mohammad, *The Contribution of Lucknow to Urdu Language and Literature*, Lucknow, 1952.

Hasani, Syed Mohammad Yunus, *Akhtar Shirani and Modern Urdu Literature*, Vikram, 1966.

Hashmi, Nurul Hasan, *Delhi ka Dabistan-e-Shairi*, Aligarh, 1943.

Hashmi, Qutub-Un-Nissa Begum, *Urdu Safarname*, Nagpur, 1959.

Husain, Mirza Sharafat, *Contribution of Maulana Azad to Urdu Literature*, Delhi, 1966.

Hussain, S.S., *A Comparative and Analytical study of women short story writers in Urdu, 1936—1960*, Ranchi, 1968.

Husain, Syed Aejaz, *Influence of Religion on Urdu Poetry, 1707—1857*, Allahabad, 1946.

Husain, Syed Fida, *A Comparative study of Firdausi and Anees*, Lucknow, 1963.

Husain, Syed Sulaiman, *Masnavis of Lucknow school of poetry*, Lucknow, 1964.

Islam, Khurshidul, *Ghalib ka ibtidai daur*, Aligarh, 1954.

Jafar, Syeda, *The Development of essay in Urdu Literature*, Osmania, 1959.

Jain, Gyan Chand, *Northern India Urdu fiction up to 1870*. Allahabad, 1948.

Jazbi, Moin Ahsan, *Political Consciousness in the poetry of Hali*, Aligarh, 1957.

Kamil, Syed Assadullah, *Sirate-nabavi: A historical and critical Evaluation*, Kashmir, 1968.

Karwani, Asafjah, *Iqbal's Philosophy of ego: Its Sources and Purpose*, Allahabad, 1956.

Khalil, Mohd. Abdul Ahad Khan, *Fifty years of Urdu Ghazal from Hali up to Akbar, 1870 A.D. - 1920 A.D.*, Lucknow, 1960.

Khan, Abdul Wadood, *Adab-e-lateef in Urdu prose*, Vikram, 1961.

Khan, Aqila Nazir Ahmed, *Akbar Allahabadi: His life and works*. Bombay, 1956.

Khan, Ebadat Yaar, *The Development of Urdu Criticism*, Lucknow, 1948.

Khan, Ghulam Mustafa, (1) *Hali ka Zehni irtika;* (2) *Farsi per Urdu ka asar;* and (3) *Ilmi nukush*, Nagpur, 1959.

Khan, Ghulam Omar, *Iqbal's Concept of Superman*, Osmania, 1956.

Khan, Masood Husain, *Urdu Zubaan kee ibtida aur irtiqa*, Aligarh, 1945.

Khan, Tauqees A., *Iqbal ki shairi mein imagery*, Delhi, 1985.

Khanum, Yasmin, *Contribution of the Department of Urdu*, Osmania University to Urdu Language and Literature, Osmania, 1987.

Madani, Syed Zahiruddin Syed Hamiduddin, *The Urdu poets of Gujarat: The Origin of Urdu Language and account of poets of Gujarat in Urdu from 900 A.H. to 1350*, A.H., Bombay, 1948.

Mannan, A., *Mir Ammen of Delhi and his Contribution to Urdu Prose*, Calcutta, 1979.

Masihuzzaman, Syed, *The Marsiya in Lucknow up to Anees*. Allahabad, 1967.

Meharunnisa, *Origin and Development of Deccani Urdu*, Osmania, 1968.

Nawvi, Manzar Abbas, *Maulana Wahiduddin Salim: Life and Work*, Aligarh, 1963.

Naqavi, Syed H.A., *Shurai-e-Urdu ke tazkirey, tanqeedi-otehqiqi mutalia: Mir se Shefta tak*, Vikram, 1968.

Naqvi, Syed Nasir Husain, *Development of Essay in Urdu*. Allahabad, 1958.

Nayyar, Iqbal, *Urdu qawaid navisi kee tarikh*, Aligarh, 1968.

Ozair, Mohammad, *Gair Islami Mazahib aur unke ikhlaq ke maqbool banane mein Urdu ka hissa*, Aligarh, 1948.

Peerzada, S. Sharfuddin, *Critical study of Illustrious Sufi Shora of the Deccan*, Seva Sadan College, Burhanpur, 1989.

Quraishi, Akbar Hussain, *A Critical study of Allusions in Iqbal's poetry*, Aligarh, 1957.

Rahman, Azizur, *Urdu Mein Seerat Nigari*, BHU, 1987.
Rizvi, S. Firasat Aslam, *The Phonetic and Phonological Structure of Standard Urdu*, Aligarh, 1968.
Rizvi, Saiyed Ahmad, *Bahadur Shah Zafar and his works*, Allahabad, 1967.
Rizvi, Saiyid Mahmoodul Hasan, *Nature and Development of Psychological Criticism in Urdu Literature*, Lucknow, 1967.
Rizvi, Saleem Hamid, *Urdu adab kee taraqqi mein Bhopal ka hissa*, Agra, 1959.
Rizvi, Syed Mohd., Aquil, *Development of Urdu Masnavi in Northern India 1750—1950*, Allahabad, 1955.
Raffiuddin, Syed, *Natia Shairi in Urdu*, Nagpur, 1956.
Rastogi, Tara Charan, *Western Influences in Iqbal*, Gauhati, 1968.
Raza, Jafar, *Contribution of Mir Ishq and his Descendants to Urdu* Marsiya, Allahabad, 1966.
Raza, Masoom, *Reflections of Indian Life as depicted in Tilism-e-Hoshruda*, Aligarh, 1964.
Rizwanullah, M., *Maulana Mohammed Anwar Shah Kashmiri: His Life and Works*, Aligarh, 1966.
Salam, Abdus, *Urdu shairi mein manzar nigari*, Lucknow, 1964.
Salam, Abdus, *Urdu Rubaiyat*, Lucknow, 1957.
Sani, Zarina Fatemi, *Seemab as nazm-writer*, Nagpur, 1969.
Sattar, Qazi Abdul, *Pessimism in Urdu Poetry*, Aligarh, 1958.
Shahid, Syed Ahmad Hussaini, *Contribution of Aminuddin in Ala and his disciples to the Deccani Literature*, Osmania, 1967.
Shakeel, A. Gaffar, *The Phonology and Morphology of Deccani Urdu as spoken in Mysore*, Aligarh, 1969.
Sharif, Jamal, *Development of Urdu poetry in Deccan before Wali*, Aligarh, 1968.
Sharifuddin, Syed Yousuf, *The Urdu novel in 20th century*, Osmania, 1968.
Shuttari, Syed Hameed, *A Critical study of the Urdu Translations and Interpretations of Quran up to 1914 A.D.*, Osmania, 1970.
Siddiqi, Shujaat Ali, *Hali as a poet*, Lucknow, 1960.
Siddiqi, Azim-u-Shan, *Growth and development of Urdu novel during 1857 to 1914*, Delhi, 1970.
Siddiqui, Abdul Haq, *Iqbaliat ka tanqeedi jaeza*, Gorakhpur, 1965.
Siddiqui, Aftab Ahmad, *Shibli aur unki tasaneef*, Aligarh, 1948.
Siddiqui, Musahib Ali, *Allusions in Urdu Literature*, Lucknow.

Singh, Mohan, *Characteristics and Tendencies of Modern Urdu poetry*, Calcutta, 1931.

Singh, S.L., *Abdur Rahman Khan Khanna: A Critical study of his life and works based on Original Sources*, Lucknow, 1952.

Soni, Barkat Ram, *Origin and Development of the Social novel in Urdu Literature*, Poona, 1962.

Srivastava, T.A., *Influence of English Literature on Modern Urdu poetry*, Agra, 1963.

Sultana, Rafia. *The Development of Urdu prose before Fort William College*, Osmania, 1955.

Ummihani, Fakhruzzaman, *Quran ka Tariq-e-Istillal (Urdu)*, Aligarh, 1969.

Wasey, Abdul, *The origin and Development of Urdu Biography writing in Qadri Bihar*, Bihar, 1969.

Yusuf, Khalida, *The Development of Urdu Literature in Aurangabad*, Osmania, 1959.

CITIES OF HISTORICAL IMPORTANCE

Agra

Agra (Pin 282 001) is a city in Western Uttar Pradesh on the south bank of the river Yamuna (Population 700,000: Muslims 16%). The history of this place is linked with that of Lodis and Mughals in India, mainly in the 16th and 17th centuries. Agra remained as capital of India during these centuries.

One can stay in Hotel Lauries* (Mahatma Gandhi Road), Hotel Grand** (Cantt. Station road), Hotel Galaxy Agra*** (Taj Ganj) etc. Like most of the military based cities in India, Agra too has a Agra Fort Railway Station and Agra Cantonment Railway Station. The most convenient train, and easily reachable place to Agra, is from Delhi. This is called Taj Express which makes a daily up and down trips. The

* 5 km from Airport, 3 km from railway station.

** 5 km from Airport, 1 km from railway station.

*** 8 km from Airport, 4 km from railway station.

distance is four hours' run. Lucknow is eight hours by train. Agra is on Bombay-Delhi, Delhi-Madras line, and hence all trains going towards South India from Delhi cross Agra. Agra is linked equally well by Air. The buses ply from Idgah bus station.

Places of interest include the most famous Moghul monument — The Taj Mahal, Akbar's Tomb at Sikandra, the structures within the Agra Fort — Jama Masjid, Moti Masjid, Khas Mahal, Diwan-i-Am, Diwan-i-Khas, Shish Mahal, etc. and Fatehpur Sikri.

Banks: Punjab National Bank, Central Bank of India, Allahabad Bank, Union Commercial Bank, Bank of India, State Bank of India, Canara *Bank*, Federal Bank, etc.

Ajmer

Ajmer (Pin 305 001) is a town in the middle of the State of Rajasthan (Population 2,80,000: Muslims 11%).

The city was a Muslim military base used in operations against the Rajputs.

By train it is both on Ahmedabad-Delhi and Udaipur-Delhi route. Ajmer is 138 km from Jaipur, 217 km from Udaipur, 441 km from Delhi and 491 km from Ahmedabad. By air one can reach Jaipur and travel from there by bus easily.

Places of interest are Mosques, White marble tombs of Khaja Muinuddin Chishti, and the palace of Akbar, now a museum.

Banks: Union Bank of India, Vijaya Bank, Indian Bank, Indian Overseas Bank, State Bank of India, Punjab National Bank, Bank of Rajasthan, etc.

Ahmedabad

Ahmedabad (Pin 380 001) (Population 2,00,000: Muslims 20%). While Ahmedabad is only a principal city of Gujarat, the capital city of Gujarat is 23 km away from Ahmedabad. Historically, it was founded in 1411 by Ahmed Shah.

---

* 11 km from Airport, 3 km from railway station.

** 10 km from Airport, 6 km from railway station.

*** 10 km from Airport, 3 km from railway station.

Places of stay include Cama Hotel* (Khanpur Road), Hotel Natraj** (Ashram Road) and Hotel Ritz*** (Lal Darwaza).

To travel to Ahmedabad by train one has to spend 24 hours from Delhi, nine hours from Bombay, 15 hours from Jaipur (the Pink City of India) and from Hyderabad. Strangely this industrial city (Manchester of the East) is not on the main broad gauge line between Delhi and Bombay and hence the absence of fast train. Bus services do exist. Air links are quite satisfactory, from Jaipur, Jodhpur (both in Rajasthan), Bombay and Delhi.

Its is a city full of fine examples of Islamic architecture. Its is a city of Mosques, like Hyderabad, but far more splendid in style and design. Prominent and noteworthy Mosques are Jama Masjid and Sidi Saiyad Masjid. A few mosques have shaking minarets (*Jhulti Minar*) and to name these: Jama Masjid; Sidi Bashir Masjid, etc. Among the Tombs are that of Ahmed Shah, Peer Mohammed Shah, and so on. *Baolis* or wells and lake are other significant areas of interest.

Banks: Punjab National Bank, Hindustan Commercial Bank, Dena Bank, Bank of Baroda, State Bank of Jaipur, etc.

Ahmadnagar

Ahmednagar (Pin 414001) (Population 1,30,000 : Muslims 20%) is a city in the State of Maharashtra. Formerly Bhinar, it was conquered by the Bahmani's in 1310, and renamed Ahmednagar by Malik Ahmed Nizam in 1490, who was the founder of Ahmednagar dynasty.

By road it is between Pune and Aurangabad. By train it is between Daund and Manmad. It is preferable to fly or travel to Pune and then reach this place which involves travelling only 82 km. Indirectly it is connected by rail and road from Bombay, Sholapur and Hyderabad.

Ashoka Tourist Hotel (Kings Gate), access 3 km from Railway station, 1 km from downtown area is a good place to stay.

Prominent historical sites are Ahmed Nizam Shah's fort, Mughal palace and gardens.

Banks: New Bank of India, Vijaya Bank, Dena Bank, State Bank of India, Bank of Baroda, Central Bank of India, Punjab National Bank, etc.

Aligarh

Aligarh (Pin 202001) is a small town of Uttar Pradesh (Population 2,80,000 : Muslims 26.6%) lies famous since a century for the first Muslim University in India a leading modern institution on western lines. Formerly know as Koil, its later name was given in 1778 during muslim rule. Interestingly Aligarh, translated as the high fort, etymologically is a mixture of Arabic and Hindustani (Ali = high; and garh = fort, respectively).

Its accessibility is most convenient from Delhi (being 126 km away), and is on the Delhi-Howrah railway route. By road it is on the Ghaziabad route.

The University guest house is one main attraction with its muslim hospitality. The places of interests are the Aligarh (fort), Dor fortress, (with an 18th century mosque) and tombs of several muslim saints.

Banks: Union Bank of India, United Commercial Bank, Vijaya Bank, Bank of Baroda, State Bank of India, Bank of India, Indian Overseas Bank, etc.

Allahabad

Allahabad (Pin 211001) is an important town of U.P (Population 6,00, 000 : Muslims 23.8%). Standing on the site of the city of Prayag, it was founded in 1583 during Akbar's regime and named as Ilahabad, "City of God". It was a provincial capital in the Mughal Empire.

Allahabad is also a significant place as it has the Nehru family home.

A place to reside in this city is the Hotel Yatrik* (S.P. Marg, Civil Lines), or Barnett Hotel** (M.G. Road). Allahabad is four hours' run by rail from Banaras, nine hours from Delhi and five hours from Lucknow. The outsider will be chased from pillar to post as there are three stations in the city. Air and bus links are satisfactory.

Places of historical interest in this town are the Fort built by Akbar, Jamia Masjid, Khusru Bagh and the Sangam (meeting points of rivers : Ganges and Yamuna (Jumna), and invisible Saraswati.

Banks: State Bank of India, Central Bank of India, Indian Bank,

* 10 km from Airport, 1/2 km from Railway Station.

** 10 km from Airport, 1 km from Railway Station.

Indian Overseas Bank, Union Bank of India, Punjab National Bank, United Commercial Bank, Allahabad Bank, Bank of Baroda, Dena Bank etc.

Aurangabad

Aurangabad (Pin 431002) (Population 175,000 : Muslims 40%) is a town of Maharashtra (formerly Khadke). Founded by Malik Amber in 1610, its present name was changed by Aurangzeb, the Mughal Viceroy, who built the Bibika Makbara tomb (in memory of his favourite wife Rabia). This tomb is reported to be an imitation of his father's Taj Mahal. Aurangabad remained for a while headquarters of the independent Nizams (of Hyderabad), but it declined when the capital was moved to Hyderabad.

Government Holiday Camp or Kathiawad Hotel or Ajanta Ambassador can provide a space for comfortable stay. This city is linked by airways, between Bombay and Delhi and a railway from Mysore in the south to Bombay in the West, Delhi in the North, Calcutta in the East is linked through Hyderabad. Bus services are fairly better to reach places within the State of Maharashtra or out.

Aurangabad, as said above, had its Muslim glorious age and resultingly there are some specimens of Islamic architecture. The Bibi-ka-maqbara is the only example of Moghul style on the Deccan Plateau. The others are *Panchakki* (water mill) fort at Daulatabad, Rauza of Aurangzeb (Khuldabad).

Banks : Central Bank of India, Bank of India, Canara Bank, Bank of Baroda, Dena Bank, Bank of Maharashtra, State Bank of Hyderabad, etc.

Bareilly

Bareilly (Pin 243001) is a historical capital of the Rohilkhand region presently in Uttar Pradesh (Population 3,60,000 : Muslims 33%).

Found in 1537 this city was built largely by the Mughal Governor Makrand Ray, when it went under a migrant clan called Rohillas, the ruler of Oudh conquered it. This city was a centre of the 1857 Sepoy Mutiny.

By train and road, it is on the Delhi-Lucknow route, and is 209 km away from Delhi.

Hotel Oberoi Anand* (Civil Lines), Civil and Military Hotel** (Jn. Station) are better places to stay.

Bareilly contains a number of fine mosques, a fort and other structures.

Banks : Union Bank of India, Vijay Bank, Oriental Bank of Commerce, State Bank of India, Allahabad Bank, Indian Overseas Bank, etc.

Bijapur

Bijapur (Pin 586101) is the former capital of Adil Shahi's (for 2 centuries, 16th & 17th) (Population 1,20,000 : Muslims 30%). Bijapur emerged as independent state after the fall of Bahmani Kingdom in 1482 A.C. The other four splinter states include Ahmednagar, Berar, Bidar and Golconda. Presently it is a town in Karnataka State.

Hotel Mayur Adil Shahi** (Anandmahal Road), Hotel Tourist (Gandhi Road), or Mysore Lodge (Station Road), or Tourist Home of Karnataka State Tourism (Station Road) are places for stay while in Bijapur. No air links exist. Train and bus network exist between Bombay, Hyderabad and Bangalore.

Architecturally Bijapur is called as Agra of the South India. Its graceful monuments include Golgumbaz, Ibrahim Roza, Jamia Masjid, Asar Mahal, Citadel, Malik-e-Maidan Cannon Upli Bruj, Mecca Masjid and others.

Banks : State Bank of India, Punjab National Bank, Canara Bank, Syndicate Bank, etc.

Bhopal

Bhopal (Pin 462003) (Population 4,25,000 : Muslims 18%) is the capital of Madhya Pradesh. This princely state was founded in 1723 by Dost Mohammed Khan (an Afghan Adventurer). Historically, Bhopal was the second largest Muslim principality of the British Empire.

Air links are from Delhi and Bombay. Being in central India it is a

* 3 km from railway station.

** 10 km from Airport, close to the railway station.

* 1 km from railway station.

link stations for trains from North to South. But same is not the case if one is travelling from East to West of the country. By road, if one has facility to travel, Bhopal lies on the Bombay-Gwalior route. Bhopal is 741 km from Delhi and 874 km from Bombay.

Jahan Numa Palace Hotel* (Shamla Hills), Hotel Ramsons International** (Hamidia Road) Nalanda Hotel*** (Ibrahimpura Street No. 2), can be opted for stay.

Places of interest are Tajul Masjid (the largest mosque in India) Jama Masjid, Moti Masjid, Idgah Hill, Islampur, etc.

Banks : Union Bank, Indian Bank, New Bank of India, Punjab National Bank, State Bank of India, Central Bank of India, Dena Bank, etc.

Bider

Bidar (Pin 585401) is a small town in Karnataka (Population 7,47,000 : Muslims 27%). History has Bidar has as a state which emerged after the fall of the Bahmani Kingdom. The independent Sultanate which emerged in 1531 was Bamaid Shahi Dynasty. Bidar lost its independence and was annexed by Bijapur in 1619-20, and a little later by Hyderabad in 1724. After partition and in the diversion of states, the town was brought under Karnataka State.

Bidar is in easy reach from Hyderabad by bus. Train facility does exist, but is not a preferred vehicle.

One may find the Tourist Home of Karnataka State Tourism or Venkateshwara Lodge or Kalpana Hotel as convenient place to rest in.

Bidar has Rangmahal (Painted Palace), Chini Mahal, remaining parts of Mahmud Gawani's Madrasa Tombs of the 12 Bahmani rulers, Ahmed Shah Bahmanis triple moat fortress, royal necropolis of the Barid Sultans, etc.

Banks : State Bank of India, Syndicate Bank, Canara Bank, State Bank of Hyderabad, Karnataka Bank, etc.

* 12 km from Airport, 5 km from railway station.

** 8 km from Airport, 2 km from railway station.

*** 7 km from Airport, 2-1/2 km from railway station.

Delhi

Delhi (Pin 110001) (Population, Chandni Chowk, Delhi East & Delhi West 16.43 lakhs : Muslims 19.1%). The old Delhi, is not one but seven cities which Hindu and Muslim Emperors gave to India. The new, the eighth Delhi, Lutyens gave India. Away from New Delhi, the old Delhi, a garden city, is always present and is one of the World's most elegant capitals.

While Delhi was not always the capital of India, it did play an important history in the annals of Indian history. This city was almost and for most of the time capital of Moslem India between the 12th and 19th centuries. Hence its historic past is blend with its vibrant past, in it being the capital of India.

Places to stay in Delhi can be Ashok Hotel* (Chanakyapuri) Hotel Flora** (Daryaganj), Hotel Metro*** (Connaught Circus) and Hotel Regal# (S.P. Mukherjee Marg).

Delhi is a major travel gateway of the country and is linked by air and rail from all the major cities of India.

Places of interest include Firozshah Kotla, Hauz Khas; Tomb of Nizamuddin Aulia, Humayun Lodi's, Safdarjang, Mosques like Jama Masjid, Khirki Masjid, Mothi ki Masjid; palaces and forts like Purana Qila, Red Fort, Shammi Talab & Jahaz Mahal and Tughlakabad, Qutub, Alai Darwaja, are some other places of interest.

Faizabad

Faizabad (Pin 224001) is a famous town, six km away from Ayodhya, the Babari Masjid-Ram Janam Bhoomi controversial site. Situated in U.P., Faizabad was founded by Sadat Ali Khan, the first Nawab of Oudh in 1730 and was capital of Muslim Rulers of Oudh. In 1775 the capital was moved to Lucknow. (Population 1,20,000 : Muslmis 30%).

Geographically it is situated on the national highway of Gorakhpur-Lucknow, and Allahabad-Faizabad railway route. From Lucknow it is 129 km and from Allahabad it is 157 km. The nearest

* Access 18 km from Airport & 9 km from New Delhi Rly. Stn.

** Access 15 km from Airport, 3 km from Rly. Station.

*** Access 14 km from Airport, 1-1/2 km from New Delhi Rly. Station.

Access 22 km from Airport, 2 km from Delhi Rly. Station.

Airport is at Lucknow.

The city has a museum, a fort built by Nawab Shuja-ud-Daulah in 1764, the tombs of his and his wife, etc.

Banks : Central Bank of India, Bank of India, State Bank of India, Punjab National Bank, Allahabad Bank, Bank of Baroda, etc.

Gulbarga

Gulbarga (Pin 585101) a town in State of Karnataka, was the first capital of the Bahmani Kingdom. It was originally in the territory of the Kakatiyas of Warangal. The Muslim connection continued from 14th century under one or the other Muslim rulers till 1948 (Population 1,60,000 : Muslims 25%).

Gulbarga is easily accessible both by train and by bus. Gulbarga is 175 km from Hyderabad.

The town is developing fastly, and it should not be difficult for one to find one such moderate lodge on station road or in the Gunj Area.

Its historic is evident from tombs of Bahmani Kings, a mosque (said to be modelled upon that of Cordoba in Spain) ; fort, the tomb of Khwaja Gesuderaz, etc.

Banks : Central Bank of India, Vijaya Bank, Karnataka Bank, Punjab National Bank, State Bank of Hyderabad, etc.

Hyderabad

Hyderabad (Pin 500001) is presently the capital of Andhra Pradesh and has had Muslim connection since 16th century. The city being fifth largest in the country, was founded in 1589, by fifth King of Qutub Shahi Dynasty Mohammed Quli (Population 2,200,000 : Muslim 40%).

Its Moghul grandeur lies side by side with modernity – a beautiful confluence of cultures. While for name-sake there are twin cities – Hyderabad and Secunderabad – but for all practical purposes any outsider can call this area as Hyderabad (These two separate towns are in a single municipality – Municipal Corporation of Hyderabad).

Air, rail and bus are well connected in the Indian travel routes. Hyderabad is 1675 km from Delhi, 800 km from Bombay, 510 km from Madras and 600 km from Bangalore. By air and train Hyderabad has direct connection from Delhi, Bombay, Calcutta and Madras, the four major cosmopolitan cities. Buses directly ply on a daily basis from

Bombay, Madras and Bangalore.
Hotel Basera* (Sarojini Devi Road, Secunderabad), Hotel Taj Mahal** (King Kothi Road, Abid road cross, Hyderabad) Asian Lodge*** (Nampally station) are good places for stay.

Places of interest are : Charminar, Mecca Masjid, Golconda Fort, Qutub Shahi Tombs, Naubat Pahad, Salarjung Museum, Himayat Sagar, Osman Sagar, Mir Alam Tank, Bagh-e-Aam, Osmania University, Falaknuma Palace, etc.

Banks : State Bank of India, Canara Bank, State Bank of Hyderabad, Syndicate Bank, Bank of Baroda, Grindlay's Bank, Andhra Bank Indian Overseas Bank, etc.

Jaunpur

Jaunpur (Pin 222001) is situated in U.P and is geographically 58 km away from Varanasi. Of the Tughluq's Firoz Shah founded Jaunpur in 1360 and was successively ruled by Sharqui's and Moghuls (Population 85,000 : Muslims 30%).

While Varanasi (formerly Banaras) is well connected by Air, rail and bus services all over the country, Jaunpur is easily accessible only via Varanasi. By train Allahabad is 115 km and Kanpur is equally distant.

Jaunpur contains several old mosques – including the Atala Masjid and the Jami Masjid ; a splendid bridge (for 16th century) called the Shahi bridge, etc.

Banks : Union Bank of India, State Bank of India, Central Bank of India, New Bank of India, Punjab National Bank, Union Bank of India, Allahabad Bank, Bank of Baroda, Banaras State Bank, etc.

Lucknow

Lucknow (Pin 226001), the capital of Uttar Pradesh (Population 9,00,000 : Muslims 29%) is principal Indian Shiite city. The Muslim

* 3 km from Airport, 2 km from Secunderabad railway station, 10 km from Hyderabad (Nampally) station.

** 2 km from Hyderabad station, 9 km from Airport and 7 km Secunderabad station

*** Opposite Hyderabad station, 11 km from Airport and 9 km from Secunderabad station.

14 km from Airport, 5 km from railway station.

rulers (Nawabs) (1724–1857) of this land too were Shiite.

One can stay at Tourist Bunglow* (Hazratganj), Avadh Lodge (Ram Mohan Rai Marg) or at Plaza Hotel, Hewett Road), Nadvat ul Ulema, situated next to Lucknow University has its own guest house.

Lucknow is only four hours distance by train from Banaras, nine hours from Agra and seven from Delhi. Being capital city it has fairly good air travel facility. As any other ordinary city in the North, there is not much of easy facility to travel by bus. Nevertheless, Charbagh bus stand, nearby the railway station, is the starting and terminating point for buses to Delhi, Agra, Allahabad, etc.

The important historical monuments are Jamia Masjid, Baradari, Imam-baras (like Shah Najaf, Hussainabad, etc.), Sikandarbagh Tombs of Ibrahim Chishti, Saadat Ali, etc., and Rumi Darwaza.

Banks : Union Bank of India, Vijaya Bank, Indian Overseas Bank, State Bank of India, Allahabad Bank, etc.

Murshidabad

Murshidabad (Pin 742149) is situated in West Bengal (Population 18,000 : Muslims 56%). Originally called Makshudabad, it was founded by Akbar. The present name was given by the Nawab Murshid Quli Khan who transferred the capital there from Dacca and thereafter remained a prominent seat of the Nawabs of Bengal.

To travel to this place it is only 221 km Northwards from Calcutta's Sealdah Station (six hours' distance by train). By road it is on a 12 km duration from the national highway of Calcutta-Baharampur (also called Berhampore).

To stay in, Hotel Historical (near Palace) or West Bengal Tourism Corporation's Tourist Lodge (in Berhampore) are appropriate.

Places of interest are Italian style Palace – Nizamat Qila, Sirajud-Daula's Tomb at Kushbagh, Moti Jhil (Pearl lake), Muradbagh Palace, etc.

Banks : State Bank of India, United Commercial Bank, Bank of India, Bank of Baroda, etc.

Patna

Patna (Pin 800001) is capital city of Bihar (Population 600,000 :

* 5 km from Airport, 2 km from railway station.

Muslims 9%) and was formerly called Patliputra, the capital of Ashoka the Great. The city was founded by an Afghan ruler in 1541 and remained prosperous during the Mughal rule.

One can stay at Hotel Rajkumar* (Exhibition Road), Hotel Park (Fraser Road) and Hotel Patliputra Ashok* (Been Chand Patel Path). The Khuda Bakhsh Oriental Public Library has its own guest house, hostel and accommodation. [9]

Patna is accessibly easily from Calcutta (Howrah) in eight hours by train. It is 16 hours journey from Delhi and only half this distance from Lucknow. Air travel is equally linked from Delhi, Calcutta, Lucknow or Kathmandu. There is bus service too.

The orientalist have their interest in Patna in the Khuda Bukhsh Oriental Library. Other places of interest in this ancient city are Sher Shahi Mosque, Pathar ki Masjid, the Madrasa on the river bank and the Golghar.

Banks : Bank of India, State Bank of Bikaner, United Commercial Bank, State Bank of India, Union Bank of India, etc.

Rampur

Rampur (Pin 244901) (Population 1,80,000 : Muslims 75%). Rampur is a part of U.P and a former capital of the Rohilla Kingdom (an Afghan dynasty).

Rampur is situated on the Amritsar-Mughalsarai railway line. It is also on the Bareilly-Moradabad National Highway. It is 617 km from Mughalsarai by train.

Hotel Tourist (Station road civil lines) is close to the station where one can stay.

Places to see are Jamia Masjid, State Library (Raza Library), Bazaars, etc.

Banks : Bank of India, Union Bank of India, Central Bank of India, State Bank of India, Allahabad Bank, Bank of Baroda, etc.

Vellore

Vellore (Pin 632001) is a town in North Arcot District of Tamil Nadu (Population 1,50,000 : Muslims 22.4%). Its history has a period of Muslim rule during the successive region of Mortaza Ali, Adil Shahi's of Bijapur and Daud Khan of Delhi.

9. ** 6 km from Airport and 2-1/2 km from railway station.

Vellore is 145 km from Madras, and 200 km from Bangalore. One has to change at Katpadi (9 km from Vellore) if one is on Bangalore-Madras route. There are also buses running from Madras and Bangalore to Vellore.

Places to stay are India Lodge (Opp. Clock Tower) arc Hotel Sangeet (near bus stand).

Places of interest are the famous fort, reputed school of Islamic learning – Baquiat us-Salehat, etc.

Banks : Vijaya Bank, Union Bank of India, Andhra Bank, Indian Bank, Canara Bank, State Bank of India, Bank of India, etc.

MISCELLANEOUS CITIES

CRANGANORE (35 km away from Cochin by ferry, and 77 km by road) has the oldest Mosque in India.

NAGORE (Pin 611002) is situated nearer to Tanjavur, and in Pondicherry District of Tamil Nadu. It is resting place of Muslim Saint.

RAEBARELI (Pin 229001) is a town in U.P and is on a major road between Varanasi and Lucknow. Named for the Bhar tribe, it has a 15 century fort and other ancient buildings. It is 122 km from Allahabad.

Banks : Vijaya Bank, Union Bank of India, United Bank of India, State Bank of India, Allahabad Bank, Dena Bank, etc.

SRIRANGAPATNAM (Pin 571438) is the last resting place and seat of the short lived Hyder Ali and Tipu's rule. Situated 12 km away from Mysore is almost part of the fast expanding city. This island had large fortifications built by Haider Ali. Major parts are still surviving. Outside this enclosure is Tipu Sultan's summer palace and the garden – Darya Daulat Bagh. Built in the Indo-Saracenic style, this palace has two walls with Frescos depicting Tipu's battles with the English and French soldiers at Tipu's side. The travellers bungalow is available for stay. There are frequent buses from Mysore apart from the Mysore-Bangalore trains which halt at Srirangapatnam, at least six times a day.

ULLAL (Pin-574159) five km from Bangalore, is a resting place of Muslim Saint.

3. EXPERTS

Research Guides in Universities
Scholars/Authors

RESEARCH GUIDES AND UNIVERSITIES

Abbas, Asghar, Ph.D., Department of Urdu, Aligarh Muslim University, Aligarh-202 001, U.P.

Abbasi, M.A., Ph.D., Department of Persian, Aligarh Muslim University, Aligarh-202 001, U.P.

Abbasi, T.B., Ph.D., School of Comparative Languages, Bhopal University, Bhopal-462 026, M.P.

Abdali, M.T., Ph.D., Department of Urdu, Magadh University, Bodh Gaya-824 234, Bihar.

Abidi, A.H.H., Prof. Ph.D., Centre for West Asian and African Studies, University of Jammu, Jammu-180 001, J & K.

Abidi, S.A.H., Prof. Ph.D., D. Litt., Department of Persian, Delhi University, Delhi-110007.

Abidi, S.Z.H., D.Phil., Department of Urdu, University of Allahabad, Allahabad-211 002, U.P.

Afsah, S.A., Ph.D., Department of Urdu, Magadh University, Bodh Gaya-824 234, Bihar.

Afzaluddin, M., Ph.D., Department of Urdu, P.G. College of Science, Saifabad, Hyderabad-500 004, A.P.

Agwani, M.S., Prof. Ph.D., Centre for West Asian & African Studies, Jawaharlal Nehru University, New Delhi-110 067.

Ahad, M.A., Ph.D., Department of Urdu, Bangalore University, Bangalore-560 005, Karnataka.

Ahmed, A.N.S., Ph.D., Department of Political Science, Dibrugarh University, P.O. Dibrugarh-786 004, Assam.

Ahmed, F., Ph.D., Department of Urdu and Persian, Rajasthan University, Jaipur-302 004, Rajasthan.

Ahmed, I., Ph.D., Department of Persian, University of Delhi, Delhi-100007.

Ahmed, I., Ph.D., Department of Political Science. Aligarh Muslim University, Aligarh-202 001, U.P.

Ahmad, Ishtiaq, Ph.D., Department of Political Science, Aligarh Muslim University, Aligarh-202 001, U.P.

Ahmad, K., Ph.D., Department of Urdu, L.N. Mithila University, Darbhanga-846 004, Bihar.

Ahmad, K. Basheer, Ph.D., Department of Arabic, Persian & Urdu, Sri Venkateshwara University, Tirupati-517 502, A.P.

Ahmad, M., Ph.D., Department of Persian, University of Bihar, Muzaffarpur-842 001, Bihar.

Ahmed, M., Prof. Ph.D., D.Litt., Department of Urdu, Patna University, Patna-800 006, Bihar.

Ahmed, M.M., Prof. Ph.D., Department of Urdu, University of Lucknow, Lucknow-226 007, U.P.

Ahmed, Mukhtaruddin, Prof. Ph.D., D.Phil., Department of Arabic, Aligarh Muslim University, Aligarh-202 001, U.P.

Ahmed, N., Ph.D., Prof. Department of Urdu, Aligarh Muslim University, Aligarh-202 001, U.P.

Ahmed, Naeem, Ph.D., Department of Urdu, Aligarh Muslim University, Aligarh-202 001, U.P.

Ahmed, Nisar, Ph.D., Reader, Department of Arabic, University of Madras, Madras-600 005, T.N.

Ahmed, Rafeek, Ph.D., Department of Political Science, University of Mysore, Mysore-570 006, Karnataka.

Ahmed, P.N., Ph.D., Department of Arabic, Persian & Urdu, University of Madras, Madras-600 005, T.N.

Ahmed, Raziuddin, Ph.D., D.Litt., Department of Arabic, Persian and Urdu, Sri Venkateshwara University, Tirupati-517 502, A.P.

Ahmed, S. Hasan, Ph.D., Department of Political Science, Aligarh Muslim University, Aligarh-202 001, U.P.

Ahmad, S.H., Prof. Ph.D., Department of Political Science, Aligarh Muslim University, Aligarh-202 001, U.P.

Ahmed, S.M., D.Litt., D.Phil., Department of Persian, University of New Delhi-110 007.

Ahmed, Samiuddin, Prof. Ph.D., Department of Persian, Aligarh Muslim University, Aligarh-202 001, U.P.

Ahmed, Shamin, Prof. Ph.D., Department of Urdu, Bhagalpur University, Bhagalpur-812 007, Bihar

Ahmad, Shamsuddin, Prof. D. Litt., Department of Persian, University of Kashmir, Srinagar-190 006, J & K.

Ahmed, Sharif, Ph.D., Department of Urdu, University of Delhi, Delhi-110 007.

Ahmed, Tanvir, Ph.D., D.Litt., Department of Urdu, University of Delhi, Delhi-110 007.

Ahmed, Z.A., D.Phil., Department of Urdu, University of Allahabad, Allahabad-211 002, U.P.

Ahmadullah, M., Ph.D., Department of Islamic Studies, Osmania University, Hyderabad-500 007, A.P.

Ahsan, M.Q., Prof. Ph.D., Department of Urdu, College of Commerce, Patna, 800 001, Bihar.

Ahsan, S.Z., Prof. Ph.D., Department of Urdu, T.P.S. College, Patna-800 001, Bihar.

Akhtar, S.S., Ph.D., Department of Urdu & Persian, Chatra College, Chatra, Hazaribagh-825 401, Bihar.

Akhtar, Waheed, Prof. Ph.D., Department of Philosophy, Aligarh Muslim University, Aligarh-202 001, U.P.

Alam, Javeed, Ph.D., Department of Political Science, Himachal Pradesh University, Simla-171 005, H.P.

Alam, K., Ph.D., Department of Urdu, K.L.S. College, Nawada-805 110, Bihar.

Alam, K.M.P., Prof. Ph.D., Department of Urdu, Kisam College, Sohsarai (Nalanda) 803 118, Bihar.

Alam, M., Ph.D., Department of Urdu, Aligarh Muslim University, Aligarh-202 001, U.P.

Alam, M., Ph.D. (Persian), Centre of African & Asian Languages, Jawaharlal Nehru University, New Delhi-110 067.

Alam, M., Ph.D., Department of Persian, Gauhati University, Gauhati-781 014, Assam.

Alam, Mansoor, Ph.D., Department of Urdu, H.D. Jain College, Arrah, 802 301, Bihar.

Alam, Muzaffar, Ph.D., Centre for Historical Studies, University of Jammu, Jammu-180 001, J & K.

Alquadri, S.M.H., Prof. Department of Arabic & Persian, University of Calcutta, Calcutta-700 073, W.B.

Alavi, M.R., Prof. Ph.D., D.Litt., Department of Arabic, Lucknow University, Lucknow-226 007, U.P.

Alvi, M.A., Ph.D., Department of Arabic, Aligarh Muslim University, Aligarh-202 001, U.P.

Ali, Amjad, Prof., D.Phil., D.Litt., Department of Islamic Studies, Aligarh Muslim University, Aligarh-202 001, U.P.

Ali, Hifazath, Ph.D., Department of Arabic, Nizam College, Hyderabad-500 001, A.P.

Ali, M.A., Ph.D., Department of Urdu, Osmania University, Hyderabad-500 007, A.P.

Ali, M. Athar, Prof., Ph.D., Department of History, Aligarh Muslim University, Aligarh-202 001, U.P.

Ali, Mohd. Hashim, Prof. Ph.D., Department of Urdu, Mysore University, Mysore-570 006, Karnataka.

Ali, N., Ph.D., Centre for West Asian Studies, Aligarh Muslim University, Aligarh-202 001, U.P.

Ali, S.S., Ph.D., Department of Urdu, University of Delhi, Delhi-110 007.

Ali, Syed, Prof. Ph.D., Department of Arabic. The New College, Madras-600 014, T.N.

Amin, Mohammed, Ph.D., Department of Arabic & Persian, University of Calcutta-700 073, W.B.

Amin, Shahid, D.Phil., Department of History & Culture, Jamia Millia Islamia, New Delhi-110 025.

Ansari, A.G., Prof. Ph.D., Department of Persian, Bhagalpur University, Bhagalpur-812 007, Bihar.

Ansari, G.M., Ph.D., D.Litt., Department of Persian, University of Bihar, Muzaffarpur-842 001, Bihar.

Ansari, M. Iqbal, Prof. Ph.D., Department of Islamic Studies, Aligarh Muslim University, Aligarh-202 001, U.P.

Ansari, M.M., D.Litt., Department of Arabic, Aligarh Muslim University, Aligarh-202 001, U.P.

Ansari, M.W., Prof. Ph.D., D.Litt., Department of Persian, University of Lucknow, Lucknow-226 007, U.P.

Ansari, N.H., Prof. Ph.D., Department of Persian, University of Delhi, Delhi-110 007.

Ansari, Sharifunnissa, Prof. D.Litt., Ph.D., Department of Persian, Osmania University, Hyderabad-500 007, A.P.

Ansari, Zoe, Ph.D., Department of Foreign Languages, Bombay University, Bombay-400 032, Maharashtra.

Ansanullah, Mohd., Ph.D., Department of Urdu, Aligarh Muslim University, Aligarh-202 001, U.P.

Anwaruddin, M., Ph.D. (Urdu), Centre of Regional Studies, University of Hyderabad, Hyderabad-500 134, A.P.

Anwar, S., Ph.D., Department of Urdu, University of Calcutta, Calcutta-700 073, W.B.

Arifi, Q.S.Z.A., Ph.D., Department of Urdu, University of Delhi, Delhi-110 007.

Asad, Mohd. S., Ph.D., Department of Arabic & Persian, University of Calcutta, Calcutta-700 073, W.B.

Asar, Ali, Ph.D., Department of Urdu, Postgraduate College, Hyderabad-500 001, A.P.

Ashraf, M., Ph. D., Department of History & Culture, Jamia Millia Islamia, New Delhi-110 025.

Ashraf, M.S., Ph.D., Department of Arabic, University of Delhi, Delhi-110 007.

Ashraf, S.W., Ph.D., Department of Arabic, Persian and Urdu, University of Madras, Madras-600 005, T.N.

Ashraf, Waheed, Ph.D., Prof. & Head, Department of Arabic, Persian and Urdu, University of Madras Annexe, Madras-600 005.

Ashrafi, S., Ph. D., Department of Urdu, Aligarh Muslim University, Aligarh-202 001, U.P.

Ashrafi, S.A.W., Prof. Ph.D., Department of Urdu, Ranchi University, Ranchi- 834 008, Bihar.

Ayub, Haroon, Ph.D., Department of Urdu, Panjab University, Chandigarh-160 014.

Ayyubi, N.A., Prof. Ph.D., Department of Islamic Studies, Aligarh Muslim University, Aligarh-202 001, U.P.

Azhar, Abdul Waheed, Prof. D.Litt., Centre of African & Asian Languages, Jawaharlal Nehru University, New Delhi-110 067.

Azam, J. Kausar, Prof. Ph.D., Department of Political Science, Osmania University, Hyderabad-500 007, A.P.

Azam, Syed, Ph.D., Department of History, Mansanyangohi, Mysore-570 006, Karnataka.

Azmi, I.U.M., D.Litt., Department of Urdu, University of Jammu, Jammu-180 001, J&K.

Azmi, Moinuddin, Prof. Ph.D., Department of Arabic, Central Institute of English & Foreign Languages, Hyderabad-500 007, A.P.

Azmi, S., Ph.D., Department of Islamic and Arab-Iranian Studies, Jamia Millia Islamia, New Delhi-110 025.

Badrunissa, Ph.D., Department of Urdu, Graduate College for Women, Jamshedpur, 831 001 Bihar.

Baig, M.A. Ali, Ph.D., Department of Urdu, Postgraduate College, Hyderabad-500 001, A.P.

Beg, M.K.A., Ph.D., Department of Linguistics, Aligarh Muslim University, Aligarh-202 001, U.P.

Baig, P.A., Ph.D., Department of Urdu, Osmania University, Hyderabad-500 007, A.P.

Bandyopadhyay, P., Ph.D., Department of Islamic History and Culture, University of Calcutta, Calcutta-700 073, W.B.

Bari, Abdul, Ph.D., Department of Arabic, Aligarh Muslim University, Aligarh-202 001, U.P.

Barkat, Ali, Ph.D. (Urdu), School of Punjabi Studies, G.N.D. University, Amritsar-143 005, Punjab.

Barkatali, S.F.A., Ph.D., Department of Urdu and Persian, Rajasthan University, Jaipur-302 004, Rajasthan.

Basha, Mahboob, Ph.D., Department of Urdu, Qaide Millat, College of Women, Mediwakkam, Vellachery, Madras 600 042, T.N.

Begum, Abida, Ph.D., Department of Urdu, University of Delhi, Delhi-110 007.

Begum, Fahmida, Ph.D., Department of Urdu, Bangalore University, Bangalore-560 056, Karnataka.

Begum, Jahanara, Ph.D., Department of Urdu, Institute of Correspondence and Continuing Education, Mysore-570006, Karnataka.

Begum, Quadija, Ph.D., Department of Urdu, Gulbarga University, Gulbarga-585 106, Karnataka.

Begum, Shareefunnissa, A., Prof. Ph.D., Department of Persian, Osmania University, Hyderabad-500 007, A.P.

Bilgrami, Raft, Ph.D., Department of History, Aligarh Muslim University, Aligarh-202 001, U.P.

Bilgrami, S.A.H., Prof. Ph.D., Department of Political Science, Aligarh Muslim University, Aligarh-202 001, U.P.

Bilgrami, S.J.R., Ph.D., Department of Political Science, Jamia Millia Islamia, New Delhi-110 025.

Bilquis, Maria, Ph.D., Department of Persian, Aligarh Muslim University, Aligarh-202 001, U.P.

Burke, A.K., Prof. D.Litt., Department of Arabic and Persian, University of Calcutta, Calcutta-700 073, W.B.

Burke, I.K., Ph.D., Department of Arabic, Persian and Urdu, Oriental Research Institute, University of Madras, Madras-600 005, T.N.

Chatterjee, R., Ph.D., Department of Islamic History and Culture, University of Calcutta, Calcutta-700 073, W.B.

Chaudhury, S.R., Ph.D., Department of Arabic, University of Delhi, Delhi-110 007.

Chaudhuri S., Prof. Ph.D., Department of Islamic History and Culture, University of Calcutta, Calcutta-700 073, W.B.

Chishti, I.H. Unwan, Prof. Ph.D., Department of Urdu, Jamia Millia Islamia, New Delhi-110 025.

Choudhury, N.A., Ph.D., Department of Urdu, University of Jammu, Jammu Tawi-180 001, J and K.

Dalvi, A.M.I., Prof. Ph.D., Department of Urdu, Bombay University, Bombay-400 032, Maharashtra.

Das, D., Department of Islamic History and Culture, University of Calcutta, Calcutta-700 073, W.B.

Faridi, M.U., Ph.D., Department of Urdu, University of Delhi, Delhi-110 007.

Fariq, K.A., Prof. Ph.D., Department of Arabic, Delhi University, Delhi-110 007.

Farooky M.A. Razzak, Ph.D., Department of Urdu and Persian, Gulbarga University, Gulbarga-5853 106, Karnataka.

Farooqui, N.R., D.Phil., Department of History, University of Allahabad, Allahabad-211 002, U.P.

Faruqi, Faizanullah, Ph.D., Department of Arabic, Centre of African and Asian Languages, Jawaharlal Nehru University, New Delhi-110 067

Faruqi, I.H.A., Ph.D., Department of Islamic and Arab-Iranian Studies, Jamia Millia Islamia, New Delhi-110 025.

Faruqui, N., Ph.D., Department of Arabic, Banaras Hindu University, Varanasi-221 005, U.P.

Fasihuzzama, Ph.D., Department of Urdu, S.U. College, Hilsa, 801 302, Bihar.

Fatmi, A.A., D.Phil. Department of Urdu, University of Allahabad, Allahabad-271 002 U.P.

Ghani, M.O., Ph.D., D.Litt., Department of Islamic History and Culture, University of Calcutta, Calcutta-700 073, W.B.

Gilani, Syed M. Yunus, Ph.D., Department of Islamic Studies, Kashmir University, Srinagar-190 006, J. and K.

Gorekar, Nizamuddin, Prof. Ph.D., St. Xavier's College, Bombay-400 001, Maharashtra.

Gupta, A., Prof. Ph.D., Centre for West Asian and African Studies, University of Jammu, Jammu-180 001, J and K.

Gupta, D.K., Prof Ph.D., Department of Persian, Urdu and Arabic, Punjabi University, Patiala-147 002, Punjab.

Habibunnisa, Ph.D., Department of Urdu, University College for Women, Koti, Hyderabad-500 001, A.P.

Habibuddin, S.M., Ph.D., Department of History, Bhagalpur University, Bhagalpur-812 007, Bihar.

Hadi, S. Nabi, Prof. Ph.D., Department of Persian, Aligarh Muslim University, Aligarh-202 001, U.P.

Hafiz, Md. Tahir Ali, Ph.D. (Persian), Department of Arabic, Persian and Islamic Studies, Viswa Bharati, Shantiniketan, W.B.-731 235.

Hai, A., Ph.D., Department of Urdu, University of Delhi, Delhi-110 007.

Haider, M., Ph.D., Department of History, Aligarh Muslim University, Aligarh-202 001, U.P.

Haider, S.S.G., Ph.D., Department of Urdu, J.J. College, Gaya, 823 001, Bihar.

Hamadi, H.U., Prof. Ph.D., Department of Urdu, University of Kashmir, Srinagar-190 001, J and K.

Hasan, A., D.Phil., Department of Urdu, University of Allahabad-211 002, U.P.

Hasan, A., Ph.D., Department of Urdu, S.P. Jain College, Sasaram (Rohtas), 823 115. Bihar.

Hasan, M., Ph.D., Department of Islamic History and Culture, University of Calcutta, Calcutta-700 073, W.B.

Hasan, Mahfuzul, Ph.D., Department of Urdu, S.N. Sinha College, Tekari, 824 236, Bihar.

Hasan, Mushirul, Prof. Ph.D., Department of History and Culture, Jamia Millia, New Delhi-110 025.

Hasan, Nurul, Ph.D., D.Litt., Department of Urdu, Aligarh Muslim University, Aligarh-202 001, U.P.

Hasan, Nural, Prof., D.Phil., Department of History, University of Delhi, Delhi-110 007.

Hasan, S.S. Prof. Ph.D., Department of Urdu, Lucknow University, Lucknow-220 007, U.P.

Hasan, S. Tariq, Ph.D., Department of Persian, Aligarh Muslim University, Aligarh-202 01, U.P.

Hashim, S.M. Ph.D. Department of Urdu, Aligarh Muslim University, Aligarh-202 001, U.P.

Hashmi, H., Ph.D., Department of Urdu, B.S.K. College, Maithon, Dhanbad, 826 001, Bihar.

Hashmi, H., Ph.D., Department of Urdu, University of Calcutta, Calcutta-700 073, W.B.

Hasnain, S.M., Prof. Ph.D., Department of Urdu, Magadh University, Bodh Gaya-824 234, Bihar.

Havewalla, S.J. Ph.D., (Persian) Centre of African and Asian Languages, Jawahar Lal Nehru University, New Delhi-110 067.

Huda, N., Prof. Ph.D., Department of Arabic, Persian and Urdu, Oriental Research Institute, University of Madras, Madras-600 005, T.N.

Huq, Abdul, Ph.D., Department of Urdu, University of Delhi, Delhi-110 007.

Huq, Fazlul, Ph.D., Department of Urdu, University of Delhi, Delhi-110 007.

Huq, Prof. Ph.D., Centre of West Asian Studies, Aligarh Muslim University, Aligarh-202 001, U.P.

Huq, Mushirul, Prof., Ph.D., Department of Islamic and Arab-Iranian Studies, Jamia Millia, New Delhi-110 025.

Huque, Mohd., Ph.D., Department of Philosophy, Aligarh Muslim University, Aligarh-202 001, U.P.

Huque, S., Ph.D., Department of Urdu and Persian, Ranchi College, Ranchi-834 001, Bihar.

Hussain, A., MED, Ph.D. Department of Hindi and Urdu, Annamalai University, Annamalainagar-608 027, T.N.

Hussain, A., Ph.D., Department of History, Aligarh Muslim University, Aligarh-202 001, U.P.

Hussain, Arshad, Ph.D. Department of Religious Studies, Panjab University, Patiala-147 002, Punjab.

Hussain, I., Ph.D. Department of History, Aligarh Muslim University, Aligarh-202 001, U.P.

Hussain, N., Ph.D., Department of Persian, Aligarh Muslim University, Aligarh-202 001, U.P.

Hussain, Q.A., Ph.D., Department of Urdu, Aligarh Muslim University, Aligarh-202 001, U.P.

Hussain, Q.J., Ph.D., Department of Urdu, Aligarh Muslim University, Aligarh-202 001, U.P.

Hussain, S., Ph.D. Department of Urdu, Ranchi University, Ranchi-834 008, Bihar.

Hussain, S.I., M.Th. Ph.D. Faculty of Shia Theology, Aligarh Muslim University, Aligarh-202 001, U.P.

Hussain, S.R., Ph.D., Department of Persian, Aligarh Muslim University, Aligarh-202 001, U.P.

Hussain, Sajjad, Ph.D. Department of Arabic, Persian and Urdu, University of Madras, Madras-600 005, T.N.

Hussain, Surouyya, Prof. D.Litt. Department of Urdu, Aligarh Muslim University, Aligarh-202 001, U.P.

Hussain, S.B.F., Ph.D. Centre of African and Asian Languages, Jawaharlal Nehru University, New Delhi-110 067.

Hyderi, A., Ph.D., D.Litt., Department of Urdu, University of Kashmir, Srinagar-190 206, J & K.

Ilahi, Mahmood, Prof. Ph.D., Department of Urdu, University of Gorakhpur, Gorakhpur-273 001, U.P.

Imam, F., Ph.D. D. Litt. Department of Urdu and Persian, Rajasthan University, Jaipur-302 004, Rajasthan.

Iqbal, M., Ph.D. Centre of West Asian Studies, Aligarh Muslim University, Aligarh-202 001, U.P.

Iqbal, S.M., Ph.D. Department of Urdu, Bhagalpur University, Bhagalpur-812 007, Bihar.

Ishrat, A.L., Prof. Ph.D., D.Litt. Department of Persian, Banaras Hindu University, Varanasi-221 005, U.P.

Islahi, M.A., Ph.D. Department of Arabic and Islamic Studies, University of Kashmir, Srinagar-190 006, J & K.

Islam, Z., Ph.D. Department of Islamic Studies, Aligarh Muslim University, Aligarh-202 001, U.P.

Jaffer, Sayeda, Prof., Ph.D., Department of Urdu, Osmania University, Hyderabad-500 007, A.P.

Jafri, A.Q., D.Phil. Department of Persian, Gauhati University, Gauhati-781 014, Assam.

Jafri, H.A.S., Ph.D. Department of Political Science, Aligarh Muslim University, Aligarh-202 001, U.P.

Jafri, S.A.H., Ph.D. Department of Persian, Banaras Hindu University, Varanasi-220 025, U.P.

Jahagirdar, R.G., Ph.D., Department of Persian and Urdu, Karnataka University, Dharwad-585 003, Karnataka.

Jahan, Nargir, Ph.D. Department of Persian, University of Delhi, Delhi-110 007.

Jaisi, K.A., Prof. Ph.D. Department of Islamic Studies, Aligarh Muslim University, Aligarh-202 001, U.P.

Javid, Qudos, Ph.D. Department of Urdu, University of Kashmir, Srinagar-190 006, J & K.

Karamadi, H.F., Ph.D. Department of Persian and Urdu, Karnataka University, Dharwad-585 003, Karnataka.

Kazmi, S.H.A., M.Sc. Ph.D., Centre of West Asian Studies, Aligarh Muslim University, Aligarh-202 001, U.P.

Khan, A.A., Ph.D., Faculty of Sunni Theology, Aligarh Muslim University, Aligarh-202 001, U.P.

Khan, A.N., D.Phil, Department of Urdu, University of Allahabad, Allahabad-211 002, U.P.

Khan, A.R., Prof., Ph.D., Department of History, Himachal Pradesh University, Simla-171 005, H.P.

Khan, A.R., M.Phil, Ph.D. Department of History, Indira Gandhi National Open University, New Delhi-110 001.

Khan, A.S., Ph.D. Department of Urdu, Osmania University, Hyderabad-500 007, A.P.

Khan, G.H., Ph.D. Department of Political Science, University of Kashmir, Srinagar-190 006 J & K.

Khan, H.A., Ph.D. Department of Arabic, Aligarh Muslim University, Aligarh-202 001, U.P.

Khan, I.H., M.A., M.Th., Ph.D. Faculty of Sunni Theology, Aligarh Muslim University, Aligarh-202 001, U.P.

Khan, M.A., Ph.D., PGDTA, Department of Arabic, Central Institute of English and Foreign Languages, Hyderabad-500 007, A.P.

Khan, M.A., Ph.D., Department of History, Ravishankar University, Raipur-492 002, M.P.

Khan, M.A., Ph.D., D.Th. Department of Islamic and Arab-Iranian Studies, Jamia Millia Islamia, New Delhi-110 025.

Khan, M.A., Ph.D. Department of Persian, University of Delhi, Delhi-110 007.

Kha, M.A., Prof. Department of Urdu, University of Delhi, Delhi-110 007.

Khan, M.H., Ph.D. School of Comparative Languages, Bhopal University, Bhopal-462 026, M.P.

Khan M.I., Ph.D. Department of Political Science, University of Kashmir, Srinagar-190 006, J & K.

Khan, M.M. Ph.D. Department of Political Science, Aligarh Muslim University, Aligarh-202 001, U.P.

Khan, M. Sulaiman, Prof. Ph.D. Department of Arabic, Persian and Urdu, Sri Venkateshwara University, Tirupati-517 502, A.P.

Khan, M.Z., Ph.D. Department of Political Science, Aligarh Muslim University, Aligarh-202 001, U.P.

Khan, Nadir, Ph.D. Department of Urdu, Aligarh Muslim University, Aligarh-202 001, U.P.

Khan, Ajmal P.N., Ph.D. Department of Islamic Tamil Literature, M.K. University, Madurai-625 021, T.N.

Khan, Rafaqab Ali, Ph.D. Department of History and Culture, Jamia Millia Islamia, New Delhi-110 025.

Khan, Rasheeduddin, Prof. Ph.D. Centre for Political Studies, Jawaharlal Nehru University, New Delhi-110 007.

Khan, A., Prof, Ph.D. Department of Urdu, S.S. College, Jahanabad, Gaya, 823 001, Bihar.

Khan, Z.M., Ph.D. Department of Political Science, Jamia Millia Islamia, New Delhi-110 025.

Khatun, M.I.S., Ph.D. Department of History, Gauhati University, Gauhati-781 014, Assam.

Kidwai, M.S. Prof., Ph.D. Department of Islamic Studies, Aligarh Muslim University, Aligarh-202 001, U.P.

Kirmani, M., Prof. Ph.D. Department of Persian, Aligarh Muslim University, Aligarh-202 001, U.P.

Kishore, M.A., Ph.D., Department of Political Science, Aligarh Muslim University, Aligarh-202 001, U.P.

Kulshreshtha, J.N., Ph.D. (Persian) Department of Urdu and Persian, Rajasthan University, Jaipur-302 004, Rajasthan.

Kutty, E.K.A., Ph.D. Department of Arabic, University of Calicut, Calicut-673 635, Kerala.

Lari, N.A. Ph.D. Department of Urdu, University of Gorakhpur, Gorakhpur-273 001, M.P.

Latif, S.K., Ph.D. Department of History, Aligarh Muslim University, Aligarh-202 001, U.P.

Mahmood, Tahir, Prof. Ph.D. Department of Law, Centre II, University of Delhi, Delhi-110 007.

Majeed, Akhtar, Ph.D. Department of Political Science, Aligarh Muslim University, Aligarh-202 001, U.P.

Malik, N.A., Ph.D. Department of Urdu, University of Kashmir, Srinagar-190 006.

Mallick, G.S., Ph.D. Department of Urdu and Persian, St. Columbus College, Hazaribagh, 825 301, Bihar.

Malik, Zahiruddin, Prof. Department of History, Aligarh Muslim University, Aligarh-202 001, U.P.

Mannan, Abdul, Ph.D. Department of Urdu, University of Calcutta, Calcutta-700 073, W.B.

Meerza, Kaukab Qadr S.A., Ph.D. Department of Urdu, Aligarh Muslim University, Aligarh-202 001, U.P.

Mir, A.M., Ph.D. Department of Urdu, University of Kashmir, Srinagar-190 006, J & K.

Mohideen, S.K., Ph.D. Department of Hindi and Urdu, Annamalai University, Annamalainagar-608 002, T.N.

Moinuddin, Khaja, Ph.D. Department of Political Science and Public Administration, Marathwada University, Aurangabad-431 004, Maharashtra.

Momin, M.M.I., Ph.D. (Persian) Department of Foreign Languages, University of Bombay, Bombay-400 032, Maharashtra.

Moosvi, Sireen, Ph.D. Department of History, Aligarh Muslim University, Aligarh-202 001, U.P.

Mohammed, A., Ph.D. Centre of West Asian Studies, Aligarh Muslim University, Aligarh-202 001, U.P.

Mohammed, Ghulam, Ph.D., Department of Arabic, Osmania University, Hyderabad-500 007, A.P.

Muhammed, K.M., Ph.D. Department of Arabic, University of Calicut, Calicut-673 635, Kerala.

Mujeeb, Abdul, Prof. Ph.D., Department of Arabic, Govt. Arts College for Men, Nandanam, Madras, 600 035, T.N.

Mustafa, S.M., Ph.D. Department of Urdu, Cooperative College, Jamshedpur, 831 001, Bihar.

Muzaffar, M.A., Ph.D. Department of Urdu, H.D. Jain College, Arrah, 802 301, Bihar.

Nadvi, Ehtesham, Prof., Ph.D. Department of Arabic, Calicut University, Calicut-673 635, Kerala.

Nadvi, Fazlur Rehman, Prof., Ph.D. Department of Islamic Studies, Aligarh Muslim University, Aligarh-202 001, U.P.

Nadvi, K.H., Ph.D. (Arabic) Department of Foreign Languages. University of Bombay, Bombay-400 032, Maharashtra.

Nadwi, M.R. Khan, Prof., Ph.D. Centre of West Asian Studies, Aligarh Muslim University, Aligarh-202 001, U.P.

Nadvi, Syed Ibrahim, Prof. Ph.D., Department of Arabic, Osmania University, Hyderabad-500 007, A.P.

Narang, G.C., Ph.D. Department of Urdu, University of Delhi, Delhi-110 007.

Naiyar, H.C., Prof., Ph.D. Department of Urdu, Banaras Hindu University, Varanasi-221 005, U.P.

Naeyara, Jameela B., Ph.D. Department of Urdu, Manasagangotri, Mysore-570 001, Karnataka.

Naqvi, M., Prof., Ph.D. Department of Urdu, Aligarh Muslim University, Aligarh, 202 001, U.P.

Naqvi, S.N., Ph.D. Department of History, Aligarh Muslim University, Aligarh-202 001, U.P.

Niazmand, M.S., Ph.D. Department of Persian, University of Kashmir, Srinagar-190 006, J & K.

Nikhat, S., Ph.D. Department of Urdu, University of Delhi, Delhi-110 007.

Nizami, T.A., Prof., Ph.D. Department of Political Science, Aligarh Muslim University, Aligarh-202 001, U.P.

Nizami, Z.A., Ph.D. Department of Political Science, Jamia Millia Islamia, New Delhi-110 025.

Pathan, Z.M., Ph.D. Department of History, Gulbarga University, Gulbarga-585 106, Karnataka.

Qadri, A.S.M., Prof., Ph.D. Department of Urdu, Postgraduate College, Hyderabad-500 001, A.P.

Qamarjahan, Ph.D. Department of Urdu, Banaras Hindu University, Varanasi-221 005, U.P.

Qamaruddin, M., Ph.D. Department of Islamic History and Culture, University of Calcutta, Calcutta-700 073 W.B.

Qasmi, M.A., BLSC, Ph.D. Centre of African and Asian Languages, Jawaharlal Nehru University, New Delhi-110 067.

Qayyum, A., Ph.D. Centre of West Asian Studies, Aligarh Muslim University, Aligarh-202 001. U.P.

Quasmi, S.H., Ph.D. Department of Persian, University of Delhi, Delhi-110 007.

Qureshi, Afsar, Ph.D. Department of Urdu, Aligarh Muslim University, Aligarh-202 001, U.P.

Qureshi, M.A., Ph.D. Faculty of Law, Rani Durgavati Vishwavidyalaya, Jabalpur-482 001, M.P.

Quraishi, Z.N., Prof., Ph.D. Department of Political Science, University of Delhi, Delhi-110 007.

Rafi, Ashraf, Prof. Ph.D. Department of Urdu, Osmania University, Hyderabad-500 007, A.P.

Rafeeq, Fatima, Ph.D. Department of Persian, University College for Women, Koti, Hyderabad-500 001, A.P.

Rafique, Mohd., Ph.D. Department of Philosophy, Aligarh Muslim University, Aligarh-202 001, U.P.

Rafiqui, A.Q., Prof., Ph.D. Department of History, University of Kashmir, Srinagar-190 006, J & K.

Rahim, Syed A., Prof., Ph.D. Department of Arabic, Institute of Arts and Social Sciences, Nagpur-440 001, Maharashtra.

Rahman, L., Ph.D. Department of Urdu, Bhagalpur University, Bhagalpur-812 007, Bihar.

Rahman, M., Prof., Ph.D. Department of Urdu, L.N. Mithila University, Darbhanga-846 004, Bihar.

Rahaman, M., Ph.D. Department of Arabic and Persian, University of Calcutta, Calcutta-700 073, W.B.

Rahman, S.S.M., Ph.D. Department of Urdu, S.P.M. College, Udantpuri, Biharsharif-803 101, Bihar.

Rahmathullah, A.I., Ph.D. Department of Arabic, University of Calicut, P.O. Calicut-673 635, Kerala.

Rahmathullah, M., Ph.D. Department of Arabic and Persian, University of Calcutta, Calcutta-700 073. W.B.

Rais, Ayisha, Ph.D. School of Comparative Languages, Bhopal University, Bhopal-462 026, M.P.

Rais, Qamar, Prof. Ph.D. Department Urdu, University of Delhi, Delhi-110 007.

Raja, J., Prof. D.Phil., D.Litt., Department of Urdu, University of Allahabad, Allahabad-211 002, U.P.

Rana, Shahnaz, Ph.D., Department of Urdu S.S.L.N.T. Mahila College, Dhanbad-826 001, Bihar.

Rashid, Mohamed, Prof. Ph.D. Department of Arabic, Aligarh Muslim University, Aligarh-202 001, U.P.

Raza, R.I., Ph.D. Department of Arabic, Banaras Hindu University, Varanasi-221 005, U.P.

Rizvi, Fida Abbas, Prof. Ph.D. School of Comparative Languages, Bhopal University, Bhopal-462 026, M.P.

Rizvi, M.M.S., Faculty of Shia Theology, Aligarh Muslim University, Aligarh-202 001, U.P.

Rizvi, S.I.R., Ph.D. Department of Arabic, Banaras Hindu University, Varanasi-221 005, U.P.

Rizvi, S.M.A., Prof. D.Phil. Department of Urdu, Allahabad University, Allahabad-211 002, U.P.

Rizvi, S.M.F.A., Ph.D. School of Comparative Languages, Bhopal Vishwavidyalaya, Bhopal-462 006, M.P.

Rizvi, H., D.Litt (Urdu) Centre of Regional Studies, University of Hyderabad, Hyderabad-500 134, A.P.

Rizvi, S.M.S.A., Ph.D., Department of Urdu, Panjab University, Chandigarh-160 014.

Rizvi, S.M.T., Ph.D. Department of Urdu, H.D. Jain College, Arrah, 802 301 Bihar.

Rizvi, S.S.H., Ph.D., Department of Urdu, Mohanlal Sukhadia University, Udaipur-313 001, Rajasthan.

Rizwanullah, Qari Mohamed, Prof. Ph.D., D.Litt., Faculty of Sunni Theology, Aligarh Muslim University, Aligarh-202 001, U.P.

Roy, A., D.Litt., Department of Islamic History and Culture, University of Calcutta, Calcutta-700 073, W.B.

Roy, A.C., Prof. Ph.D. Department of Islamic History and Culture, University of Calcutta, Calcutta-700 073, W.B.

Sadiq, Mohd., Prof. Ph.D., Centre for West Asian and African Studies, University of Jammu, Jammu-180 001, J & K.

Safiullah, Ph.D. Department of Arabic, Persian and Urdu, University of Madras, Madras-600 005, T.N.

Sajida, Zeenath, Ph.D. Department of Urdu, Nizam College, Hyderabad-500 001, A.P.

Sajjad, A., Ph.D., Department of Urdu, Ranchi University, Ranchi-834 008, Bihar.

Sardar, N., D.Phil, Department of Urdu, University of Allahabad, Allahabad-211 002, U.P.

Sattar, Qazi, Prof. Ph.D. Department of Urdu, Aligarh Muslim University, Aligarh-202 001, U.P.

Shaharyar, Akhlaq, Ph.D. Department of Urdu, Aligarh Muslim University, Aligarh-202 001, U.P.

Shamimuddin, Ph.D. Department of Urdu, J.S. College, Daltongunj, 822 101, Bihar.

Sharifuddin, Y., Prof. Ph.D. Department of Urdu, Osmania University, Hyderabad-500 007, A.P.

Shaukat, Sameena, Prof. Ph.D. Centre of Regional Studies, University of Hyderabad, Hyderabad-500 134, A.P.

Shirwani, R.R., Prof. Ph.D. Department of Arabic, University of Kashmir, Srinagar, 190 006, J & K.

Siddiqi, A.A. Prof. Ph.D. Department of Urdu, Aligarh Muslim University, Aligarh-202 001, U.P.

Siddiqi, A.N. Ph.D. Department of Persian, University of Kashmir, Srinagar-190 006, J & K.

Siddiqui, A.S., B.Ed., Ph.D. Department of Persian, M.S. University, Baroda-390 002, Gujarat.

Siddiqui, Asiya, Ph.D. Department of History, University of Bombay, Fort, Bombay-400 032, Maharashtra.

Siddiqui, H.A., Ph.D. Department of Arabic, Nizam College, Bashirbagh, Hyderabad-500 001, A.P.

Siddiqi, Hamra, Ph.D. Department of Urdu, University of Jammu, Jammu-Tawi-180 001, J & K.

Siddique, M., Prof. Ph.D. Department of Persian, Patna University, Patna-800 005, Bihar.

Siddiqi, M.A., Ph.D. Department of Islamic Studies, Aligarh Muslim University, Aligarh-202 001, U.P.

Siddiqui, M.H., Ph.D. Department of Persian, M.S. University, Baroda-390 002, Gujarat.

Siddiqui, M.H., Ph.D. Centre for Historical Studies, University of Jammu, Jammu-180 001, J & K.

Siddiqui, M.H.A., Ph.D., Department of Arabic, Osmania University, Hyderabad -500 007, A.P.

Siddiqi, M.K. Ph.D. Department of Persian, Aligarh Muslim University, Aligarh-202 001, U.P.

Siddiqui, M.S., D.Phil, Department of Urdu and Persian, Dr. Hadir Singh Gour Vishwavidhyalaya, Sagar-470 003, M.P.

Siddiqi, Y.M., Ph.D. Department of Islamic Studies, Aligarh Muslim University, Aligarh-202 001, U.P.

Siddiqi, N.A., Ph.D. Department of Persian, Aligarh Muslim University, Aligarh-202 001, U.P.

Siddique, S.A., Ph.D. Department of Urdu and Persian, St. Columbus College, Hazaribagh-825 301, Bihar.

Siddiqui, S.B. Ph.D. Department of Persian, M.S. University Baroda-390 002, Gujarat.

Siddiqi, Suleiman, Prof. Ph.D. Department of Islamic Studies, Osmania University, Hyderabad-500 007, A.P.

Siddiqi, Y.M., Prof. Ph.D. Department of Islamic Studies, Aligarh Muslim University, Aligarh-202 001, U.P.

Siddiqi, Z. Prof. Ph.D. Department of History, Aligarh Muslim University, Aligarh-202 001, U.P.

Siddiqui, Z.A. Prof. Ph.D. Department of Urdu, University of Delhi, Delhi-110 007.

Siddiqi, Z.S., M.Th., Ph.D., Faculty of Sunni Theology, Aligarh Muslim University, Aligarh-202 001, U.P.

Singh, Amarwant, Ph.D. Department of Persian, Urdu and Arabic, Punjabi University, Patiala-147 002, Panjab.

Singh, Attar, Prof. Ph.D. Head, Sheikh Baba Farid Chair of Medieval Indian Literature, Panjab University, Chandigarh-160 014.

Siraj, Masood, Ph.D. Department of Urdu, University of Mysore, Mysore-570 006, Karnataka.

Subhan, A. Prof. Ph.D. (Persian), Maulana Azad College, Calcutta-700 013, W.B.

Sultana, I.A., Ph.D., Department of Urdu, Nalanda Mahila College, Biharsharif, Nalanda-803 101, Bihar.

Syed, A.J., Prof. Ph.D. Department of History University of Bombay, Bombay-400 032, Maharashtra, (Specialisation Medieval Indian History).

Syed, T.A., D.Phil. Department of Arabic and Persian, University of Allahabad, Allahabad-211 002, U.P.

Tabassum, Moghani, Prof. Ph.D. Department of Urdu Osmania University, Hyderabad-500 007, A.P.

Tabish, S.A., Ph.D. Department of Urdu, University of Delhi, Delhi-110 007.

Tasneem, Almas, Ph.D. Department of Urdu, Arvind Mahila College, Patna-800 001, Bihar.

Tirmizi, B.A., Ph.D., Department of Persian, Gujarat University, Navrangpura, Ahmedabad-380 009, Gujarat.

Uganwi, M.Z., Ph.D. Department of Urdu, University of Calcutta, Calcutta-700 073, W.B.

Umar, Mohd., Ph.D. Department of History, Aligarh Muslim University, Aligarh-202 001, U.P.

Usmani, A.F., Prof. LL.B.,.Ph.D. Department of Political Science, Aligarh Muslim University, Aligarh-202 001, U.P.

Waheedi, R., Ph.D., Department of Islamic and Arab-Iranian Studies, Jamia Millia Islamia, New Delhi-110 025.

Wani, M., Ph.D. Department of Urdu, University of Kashmir, Srinagar-190 006, J & K.

Wani, M.A., Ph.D. Department of History, University of Kashmir, Srinagar-190 006, J & K.

Wasey, A. Ph.D., Department of Urdu, University of Bihar, Muzaffarpur-842 001, Bihar.

Zafar, Ahmad, Ph.D. Department of Urdu, Banaras HIndu University, Varanasi-221 001, U.P.

Zahuruddin, A., Ph.D. Department of Urdu, University of Jammu, Jammu-Tawi-180 001, J & K.

Zaibunisa, Ph.D. Department of Persian, Osmania University, Hyderabad-500 007, A.P.

Zaidi, S.M.A., Ph.D., Department of Urdu, Rajasthan University, Jaipur-302 004, Rajasthan.

Zaman, Mohd., Ph.D. Department of Urdu, University of Kashmir, Srinagar-190 006, J & K.

Zilli, Ishtiaq, Ph.D. Department of History, Aligarh Muslim University, Aligarh-202 001, U.P.

SCHOLARS/AUTHORS

Abbasi, Shahid Ali, Department of Islamic Studies, Osmania University, Hyderabad-500 007, A.P.

Abdullah, C., Ph.D., Principal, Darul Uloom Arabic College, Vazhakkad, 673 640, Kerala.

Abdus Salam, C.A. Ph.D., Pro-Vice Chancellor, Cochin University of Science and Technology, Cochin-682 022, Kerala (Islamic Sciences).

Aboobakr, K.P., M.A. Department of Arabic, University of Calicut, P.O. Calicut-673 635, Kerala.

Aboobaker, K.C. Principal, Anvarul Islam Arabic College for Women, Kondotty, 673 638, Kerala.

Ahad, Hakim Abdul, Alim Islamic Arabic and Oriental Examination and Fazil Tibb-o-Jarahat, B-8, P.C. Colony, Kankerbagh, Patna-800 020, Bihar.

Ahmed, A. Basheer, M.A. Junior's Cultural Academy, 200 Quaide Millath Road, Triplicane, Madras-600 005. T.N. (Islamic Studies, Tamil).

Ahmed, Amin, Department of Urdu, A.N.S. College, Barh.

Ahmed, Anwar, M.A. Department of Urdu, Daudnagar College, Daudnagar, 824 113, Bihar.

Ahmed, Aqil, M.A. Department of Urdu, S.N. Sinha College, Jahanabad, 804 408, Bihar.

Ahmed, Asrar, Editor, *Tahzeebul Akhlaq*, Aligarh Muslim University, Aligarh-202 001, U.P.

Ahmed, Ausaf, Ph.D. Department of Economics, Jamia Millia Islamia, New Delhi- 110 025.

Ahmad, H., M.A. Department of Arabic and Persian, University of Allahabad, Allahabad-211 002, U.P.

Ahmed, Hafiz M.A.K. Syed, 56B, Dheevu Street, Kayalpatnam, Tirunelveli Dist., 628 204, T.N. (Tamil Writer on Islam).

Ahmed, Hasnuddin, M.A. C-307, Curzon Road Apartments, New Delhi-110 004 (or Aziz Bagh, Sultanpura, Hyderabad-500 024), A.P.

Ahmad, Kalimuddin, Prof. M.A. 7B, Srikrishnapuri, Patna-800 001 Bihar (Chief Editor, Urdu-English Dictionary Project).

Ahmad, M.A. Department of Urdu, Aligarh Muslim University, Aligarh-202 001, U.P.

Ahmed, F., M.A. Department of Urdu, K.L.S. College, Nawada, 847 202, Bihar.

Ahmed, M., M.A. Department of Urdu, University of Calcutta, Calcutta-700 073, W.B.

Ahmed, Md. Ibrar, M.A. Department of Urdu, S.N. Sinha College, Jahanabad, 804 408, Bihar.

Ahmed, Mohd. Kobad Ali, Maulvi, 276 (A) Gorala Central Avenue, Gauhati, Assam-781 011 (Assamese Writer).

Ahmed, Mushtaq, M.A. Department of Urdu, Yuvaraja's College, Mysore-570 005, Karnataka.

Ahmed, N., M.A. Department of Urdu, B.S. College, Lohardaga, 835 302, Bihar.

Ahmed, O.S., M.A. Department of Urdu, Ranchi University, Ránchi-834 008, Bihar.

Ahmed, P. M.A. Department of Urdu, Sheodani College, Kaler, Gaya, 824 127, Bihar.

Ahmad, Q.M., Prof. Ph.D. Head, Department of Geography, Jamia Millia Islamia, New Delhi-110 025.

Ahmed, S., M.A. Department of Urdu, S. Sinha College, Aurangabad, 824 101, Bihar.

Ahmed, S.A., M.A. Department of Urdu, A.M. College, Gaya, 823 001, Bihar.

Ahmed, S.H. Department of History, University of Delhi, Delhi-110 007.

Ahmed, Shafique, M.A. Department of Urdu, S.S. College, Sasaram, 821 115 , Bihar.

Akbar, Md., M.A. Department of Arabic, P.G. College of Science, Saifabad, Hyderabad-500 004. A.P.

Akhter, Nurus Sayeed, Prof. Ph.D. Nishat/3, Raiswala Compound, CST Road, Kurla, Bombay-400 070. Maharashtra, (Urdu/Persian Writer).

Akhtar, Shamim, M.A. Department of Persian, Banaras Hindu University, Varanasi-221 004, U.P.

Akhtar, Y., M.A. Department of Urdu, Doranda College, Ranchi, 834 001, Bihar.

Alam, Maqsood, M.A. Department of Persian, M.S. University, Baroda-390 003 Gujarat.

Ali, B. Sheik, Prof. Ph.D. Vice Chancellor, Goa University, Goa. (Historian).

Ali, M. Abbas, Ph.D. Department of Business Management, University College of Commerce, Osmania University, Hyderabad-500 007, A.P.

Ali, M.R., M.A. Department of Arabic, Gauhati University, Gauhati, Assam-701 014.

Ali, Mohd. Haneef, Shaikul *Hadith*, 441, Bail Bagh, Malegaon-423 203, Maharashtra, (*Hadith*).

Ali, Nisar, Ph.D. Department of Economics, University of Kashmir, Srinagar-190 006, J & K.

Ali, Osman, M.Phil. Department of Urdu, Postgraduate College of Science, Secunderabad-500 003 A.P.

Ali, Rasheed, M.A. Department of Urdu, Maharaja's College, Mysore-570 005, Karnataka.

Ali, S.A., M.A. Department of History, Kakatiya University, Warangal-506 009, A.P.

Allahabadi, Aslam, Shanker Building, Mastan Tank, Bombay-400 008. Maharashtra, (Urdu Writer).

Ameeruddin, Syed, Prof. D.Litt. 14, Mirza Ghulam H.A. Khan Street, Rayapeta, Madras-600 014, T.N.

Ansari, A.A., M.A. Department of Urdu, B.S.K. College, Maithon, Dhanbad, 826 001, Bihar.

Ansari, Hayathullah, B.A. B2/4, River Bank Colony, Lucknow-226 001, U.P. (Urdu Writer).

Ansari M.N., M.A. Department of Urdu, J.J. College, Gaya, 823 001, Bihar.

Ansari, Mohd, Z., M.A., B.Lib. Sc. Muzzammil Manzil, Civil Lines, Aligarh-202 001, U.P. (Urdu Writer).

Ansari, Shahabuddin, Librarian, Dr. Zakir Husain Library, Jamia Millia Islamia, New Delhi-110 025.

Ansari, Asloob, A. Prof. M.A. Department of English, Aligarh Muslim University, Aligarh-202 001, U.P.

Ansarullah, Mohammad, Ph.D. Adib-e-Kamil, 4/585, Sir Sayed Road, Sir Syed Nagar, Aligarh, 202 001, U.P. (Compiler of bibliography, glossary, editor of magazine and writer).

Anwarudeen, M.M., 15, Mansoor Street, Titachery, Tanjavur Dist., T.N.-609 703. (Tamil Writer).

Asadullah, M. M.A., M. Th., B.lib. Sc. Faculty of Sunni Theology, Aligarh Muslim University, Aligarh-202 001, U.P.

Asadullah, U. Mohd. Prof. Ph.D. Department of English, Govt. College of Education, Madras-600 015. T.N., (Islamic Studies, Tamil).

Ashrafi, A., M.A. Department of Urdu, Ramgarh College, Ramgarh, 829 122, Bihar.

Askari, Syed Hasan, D.Litt. P.O. Mahendru, Patna-800 006. Bihar, (History).

Ataullah, M.A. Department of Urdu, J. Nehru College, Chakradharpur, 848 120, Bihar.

Ayyub, Abu Sayeed, M.A. 5, Pearl Road, Calcutta-700 017. W.B. (Writer in Bengali and English).

Azad, Ghulam Nabi, B.A. (Hons. in Urdu and Kashmiri), Yaripura, Anantnag, Kashmir,192 101 J & K.

Azeez, Abdul, Jami Umri, Prof. Boag Road, Near Anjuman-i-Himayat, Madras-600 017, T.N. (Arabic Writer).

Aziz, Abbasi, M.A. (Persian) School of Punjabi Studies, G.N.D. University, Amritsar-143 005, Punjab.

Azmi, Abdul Latif, M.A., Alim. C/o VC's Office, Jamia Millia Islamia, New Delhi-110 025. (Urdu Writer)

Azmi, Yusuf, Ph.D. Department of English, Anwarul-uloom College, Mallepally, Hyderabad-500 002, A.P.

Badeeuzaman. Mohd., Retd. Addl. Dist. Magistrate, Haroon Nagar Colony, 1st Sector, Phulwari Sharif, 801 505, Bihar.

Baig, A. Razack, M.A., M.A.,LL.B. 23-1-562, Bibi Bazar, Hyderabad-500 002, A.P.

Balkhi, I., M.A. Department of Urdu, G.L.A. College, Daltonganj, 822 101, Bihar.

Balkhi, M., M.A. Department of Urdu, J.S. College, Daltonganj, 822 101, Bihar.

Balkhi, S., M.A. Department of Urdu, S.M.S.G. College, Sherghati, 824 211, Bihar.

Bano, R., M.A. Department of Urdu, Graduate College of Women, Jamshedpur, 831 001, Bihar.

Baqavi, Syed Qudrathullah, 155, Udaygiri, Mysore-570 017. Karnataka, (Arabic/Islamic Studies).

Basheerunissa, S., M.A. Department of Persian, Osmania University, Hyderabad-500 007, A.P.

Bavakutty, M., M.Lib.Sc., M.A., Ph.D. University librarian, Calicut University, Calicut-673 635, Kerala.

Bedar, A.R., Ph.D. Director, Khuda Bhaksh Oriental Public Library, Patna-800 004, Bihar.

Begum, Shakira, M.A., B.L.Sc. Osmania University Library, Osmania University, Hyderabad-500 007, A.P.

Bhadra, G., M.A. Department of Islamic History and Culture, University of Calcutta, Calcutta-700 073, W.B

Burhanuddin, Mohamed, M.A., M.Lib.Sc. Library, University of Hyderabad, Hyderabad-500 134, A.P.

Burney, Syed, M.H., I.A.S. F3/17, Vasant Vihar, New Delhi-110 057, (Public Affairs/Social Affairs).

Prof. Chughtai, S.Z., Department of Physics, Aligarh Muslim University, Aligarh-202 001, U.P.

Chaudhury, L.R., M.A. Department of Urdu, L.B.S. Memorial College, Jamshedpur, 831 001, Bihar.

Choudhury, Khairuddin, M.A., B.T. C/o E. Chandra Singh, Banipara, Silchar, Cachar, Assam-788 001, (Writer in Manipuri, Bengali on Islam and other topics).

Dalal, Yasin, A., M.A. Aakar, Shreeji Nagar, Behind Race Course, Rajkot-360 001, Gujarat (Journalism, Gujarati Writer).

Dalvi, M.A., B.Com., M.Ed., LL.M. Ph.D. 249 Ghorpade Peth, Pune-411 042, Maharashtra (Islamic Studies, Marathi).

Dargahwala, Imamuddin, S., 335, Dargah Road, Navsari, Valsad Dist. Gujarat-396 445, (Gujarati Writer on Islam/Sufis).

Desai, Ziyauddin, Ph.D. 14, Khurshid Park, Sarkhej Road, Ahmedabad-380 055. (Persian, Archaeology).

Desnavi, A.Q., Prof. M.A. Saifia College, Bhopal-462 001, M.P. Urdu Writer on Islam and other topics).

Eisa, Mufti Mohammed, Madrasa Nusrat-ul Uloom, Gojranvala.

Engineer, Asghar, A., Ph.D. Director, Institute of Islamic Studies, 2nd Floor, 4th Road, Irene Cottage, Santacruz (East) Bombay-400 055, Maharashtra.

Fakeer, Abdul Kareem, Bana Mohalla, Razdan Lane, P.O. Habba Kadal, Srinagar, J & K., (Kashmiri Poet).

Farooqi, Aisha, M.Phil. Department of Islamic Studies, Osmania University, Hyderabad-500 007, A.P.

Farooqi, Jamil, Ph.D. Department of Sociology, Aligarh Muslim University, Aligarh-202 001, U.P.

Faroqi. M.A. Prof. Ph.D. Department of Psychology, Calicut University, Calicut-673 635, Kerala.

Farooqi, Mohd. Rafiuddin, LL.B., M.B.A., M.A. M.Phil. Farooqi Manzil, R.T.C. Cross Road, Hyderabad-500 020, (Specialisation Islamic Politics).

Farooqui, Moin, M.A. Editor Angaray, 11-2-550, Aghapura, Hyderabad.

Faruqi, N.A., M.A. Department of Arabic, University of Delhi, Delhi-110 007.

Faruqui, R.H. Department of Urdu, College of Humanitics, Udaipur, 313 001, Rajasthan.

Faruqi, Shamsur Rahman, M.A. DII/35, Kaka Nagar, New Delhi-110 003. (Director Tarraqi Urdu Board, Govt. of India).

Faruk, K. Mohd., M.A. Department of Tamil, Sadakathullah Appa College, Palayamkottai-627 002, T.N.

Fatimi, M.A.K., M.A., B.Lib. Sc. Asst. Librarian, Osmania University Library, Osmania University, Hyderabad-500 007, A.P., (Spec. Translation, Transliteration, Bibliography, Classi. Scheme C.).

Fatmi, Z., M.A. Department of Urdu, J.D.Women's College, Patna-800 001, Bihar.

Gafoor, K. Abdul, Prof. M.A., C.Lib.Sc. 'Muzzammil', Mettukadai, Thuckalay, Kanyakumari Dist.-629 175, T.N. (Islamic Studies, Tamil).

Gafoor, P.P. Abdul, Maulvi, Madeenathul Uloom Arabic College, Pullikkal, Malappuram- 670 505, Kerala.

Giazuddin, M.A. Department of Urdu, Nizam College, Bashirbagh, Hyderabad-500 001, A.P.

Hai, Abdul, Librarian, Urdu Hall Library, Urdu Arts College, Himayatnagar, Hyderabad-500 029, A.P.

Haider, M.A. Department of Urdu, Katras College, Katras, 828 114, Bihar.

Hajini, Mohiyuddin, Prof. M.A., LL.B. Hajiri, Tehsil Sonawari, Baramulla Dist. 191 203, J & K., (Arabic, Kashmiri Writer and Translator).

Haider, S.Mohd., M.A. Department of Urdu, S.B. College, Arrah-802 301, Bihar.

Hamaddi, H.U., Ph.D. Department of Urdu, University of Kashmir, Srinagar-190 006, J & K.

Hamid, A., M.A. Department of Urdu, University of Allahabad, Allahabad-211 002, U.P.

Hamid, Mohd., M.Phil. Department of Islamic Studies, Osmania University, Hyderabad-500 007, A.P.

Hamid, Syed, Prof. Ex-Vice Chancellor, Hamdard Nagar, New Delhi-110 062.

Haqni, S.H., M.A. Department of Urdu, Magadh University, Bodh Gaya-824 234, Bihar.

Hashmi, N.H., Prof. Ph.D., D.Litt. Ismail Building, University Road, Lucknow-226 007, U.P., (Urdu Writer).

Hassan, A.M., M.A. Department of Urdu, Tata College, Chaibasa, 833 201, Bihar.

Hassan, E.B., M.A., M. Th. Department of Islamic Studies, Aligarh Muslim University, Aligarh-202 001, U.P.

Hasan, M.M., M.A. Department of Urdu, S.P. Jain College, Sasaram (Rohtas)-821 115, Bihar.

Hasan, S., M.A. Centre of West Asian Studies, Aligarh Muslim University, Aligarh-202 001, U.P.

Hasan, S.M., Prof. B.Com. LL.M. Department of Law, Aligarh Muslim University, Aligarh-202 001 U.P.

Hasan, S.N. M.A. Department of Urdu, J.L.N. College, Dehri-on-Sone, (Rohatas)-821 307, Bihar.

Hasan, S.S., M.Phil. Department of Islamic Studies, Aligarh Muslim University, Aligarh-202 001, U.P.

Hasan, Syed, M.A. Singh House, Tripolia, Patna-800 007, Bihar, Persian).

Hashmi, S.A., M.A. MSLS, Dist. Librarian, Secretary, Dist. Library Authority, Adilabad-504 001, A.P.

Hassan, Ghulam Beg. M.Sc Arif Manzil, Gogi Bagh, Srinagar-190 001, J & K, (Working on a dictionary of proverbs for Kashmir University).

Hay, A. Abdul, Prof. M.A. Department of Arabic, Sadakathullah Appa College, Palayamkottai-677 002, T.N.

Hindi, A.L.Al., M.A. Department of Arabic and Persian, University of Allahabad, Allahabad-211 002, U.P.

Huda, Q., M.A. Department of Urdu, Gaya College, Gaya, 823 001, Bihar.

Huq, A., M.A. (Arabic) Centre of African and Asian Languages, Jawaharlal Nehru University, New Delhi-110 067.

Haq, M., M.A. Department of Arabic and Persian, University of Allahabad, Allahabad-211 002, U.P.

Huque, Mahmadul, Department of Urdu, J.N.L. College, Khagaul, Patna-801 105, Patna.

Huq, R., M.A. Department of Arabic and Islamic Studies, University of Kashmir, Srinagar-190 006, J & K.

Hussain, M. Sabir, Prof. M.A., M.Lib.Sc. Department of Library Science, Aligarh Muslim University, Aligarh-202 001 U.P.

Hussain, A., M.A. Department of Urdu, Aligarh Muslim University, Aligarh-202 001, U.P.

Hussain, Bashir Zaidi, D.Litt. Zaid Villa, Jamia Nagar, New Delhi-110 025.

Hussain, Hm.H.S.M. Kamaluddin, Unani Tibb and Surgery, Aligarh Muslim University, Aligarh-202 001, U.P.

Hussain, M., M.A. Department of Urdu, Women's College, Jamshedpur, 831 001, Bihar.

Hussain, M., M.A. Department of Urdu, Gaya College, Gaya, 823 001, Bihar.

Hussain, Manzer, M.A. Department of Urdu, Ramgarh College, Ramgarh, Bihar.

Hussain, Masud, Prof, Ph,D., D.Litt. Javid Manzil, Jamia Urdu Road, Civil Lines, Aligarh-202 001, U.P. (Urdu Writer and editor of several classics).

Hussain, Mir Mahmood, Prof. M.A. Chick Veeranna Rice Mill Road, Opp. Banimantap, Mysore-570 015, Karnataka, (Arabic/Persian/Islamic Studies).

Hussain, S., M.Sc., M.Lib. Sc. department of Library Science, Aligarh Muslim University, Aligarh-202 001, U.P.

Hussain, S.S., M.A. Department of Urdu and Persian, R.S.P. College, Jharia-828 111 Bihar.

Hussain, S.S., M.Phil. Department of Arabic, Persian and Urdu, Oriental Research Institute, University Of Madras, Madras-600 005, T.N.

Hussami, Maulana Aqil, Panj-e-Shah, Hyderabad-500 002, A.P.

Hussami, Maulana Jalaluddin Kamil, Panj-e-Shah, Hyderabad-500 002, A.P.

Hussami, Hakim Syed Qudrathulla, Director, Fazil Academy, Research Foundation for Islam and Medical Sciences, 22-6-785, Panj-e-Shah, Hyderabad-500 002, A.P., (Specialising in Islamic Medical Sciences).

Ibrahim, K.N., Moulvi, C/o Madeenathul Uloom, Arabic College, Pullikkal, Malappuram-676 505, Kerala.

Ilahi, Ayyub, B.I.M.S. Maqbra II, Moradabad-244 001, U.P. (Urdu Writer and Translator).

Imam, H., M.A. Department of Urdu, A.S. College, Bikramganj-802 212, (Rohtas), Bihar.

Imam, M.A. Rrof. Department of Urdu, Maharaja College, Arrah-802 301, Bihar.

Imam, Masooda, M.A. Department of Urdu, Ranchi Women's College, Ranchi-834 001, Bihar.

Imam, S.M., M.A. Department of Urdu, Jagannath Nagar College, Dhurwa, Ranchi-834 004, Bihar.

Iqbal, Syeed, Department of Sociology, Burhania College, Bombay-400 010, Maharashtra.

Iqbal, U. Mohd., Prof. Khadir Mohidden College, Adirampattinam, Tanjur Dist. - 614 701, T.N.

Islahi, Z.R. Mohd., M.A. Department of Urdu, R.L.S. Yadav College, Bakhtiarpur-803 212, Bihar.

Islam, Mohd., M.A. Department of Urdu, Bokaro Steel City College, Bokaro-827 001, Bihar.

Ismail, Ali Mohamed, M.A. 13, New Raput Block, N.R. Mohalla, Mysore-570 007, (Specialisation Arabic/Islamic Studies).

Jafri, Ali Sardar, Secta Mahal, Bomanji Patil Road, Bombay-400 036, Maharashtra, (Urdu Writer).

Jawahar, Moulana Mubarak Karim, M.Th. Alim Fazil, 2/1, Tiljala Place, P.S. Karaya, Calcutta-700 017, (Translator of *Quran*, Bengali Writer).

Kadar, A.P., Moulvi, Principal, Anwarul Islam Arabic College, Kuniyil, Kizhuparamba, Kerala.

Kader, A.P.A., C/o Ansar Arabic College, Valavannur-676 555, Kerala.

Kareem, N.K.A., Prof. Department of Islamic History, Farook College, Feroke-673 632, Kerala.

Kazimi, S.A.A., Prof. Department of Arabic, Patna University, Patna-800 005, Bihar.

Khan, A.M., MSLS, Department of Library Science, Aligarh Muslim University, Aligarh-202 001, U.P.

Khan, A. Rayees, M.A. Ph.D. A'1 Old Staff Quarters, Osmania University, Hyderabad-500 007 A.P. (Specialisation Islamic law).

Khan, A. Saleem, M.A., B.L. Sc. Librarian, Indian Institute of Islamic Studies, New Delhi-110 062.

Khan, Asadullah, M.A. Department of Urdu, A.N.S. College, Nabinagar-824 301, Bihar.

Khan, Abid Ali, B.A. Editor, *Siyasat,* Abid Manzil, 6-2-13, Saifabad, Hyderabad-500 004, A.P.

Khan, Ahmedulla, Prof. M.L., Ph.D. Department of Law, Nagarjuna University, Nagarjunasagar-522 510, A.P.

Khan, Akbar Ali, Ph.D., Department of Public Administration, Osmania University, Hyderabad-500 007, A.P.

Khan, Akhlaq M., Ph.D. G.N. Dev University Library, Amritsar-143 001, (Urdu writer and editor of magazines).

Khan, B.A., Ph.D. Department of Economics, University of Kashmir, Srinagar-190 006, J & K.

Khan, Ghouse Ahmed, Prof. Head, Department of Arabic, Wakf Board, College, Madurai-625 001, T.N.

Khan, H.A., Prof. M.Lib.Sc., Ph.D. Department of Library Science, Mysore University, Mysore-570 006, Karnataka.

Khan, Khliq, A., Ph.D., Dip. in Lib.Sc., Dip. in Ling., Anjum Lodge, Kalan Mahal, New Delhi-110 002, (Urdu Writer and Editor of Magazines).

Khan, M., M.A. Prof. Department of Urdu and Persian, Nalanda College, Bihar Sharif, Nalanda-803 101, Bihar.

Khan, M.A. Saleem, Prof. Centre of West Asian Studies, Aligarh Muslim University, Aligarh-202 001, U.P.

Khan, M.M.S., M.A. Department of Urdu, P.K.R. Memorial College, Dhanbad-826 001, Bihar.

Khan, Mansha-ur-Rehman, Ph.D., B.T. 11 Starky Town, Nagpur-440 001, (Specialisation in Urdu and Persian Literature and Urdu Writer).

Khan, Masood Ali, Ph.D. Deputy Director, ICSSR, Southern Regional Centre, Osmania University Campus, Hyderabad-500 007, A.P.

Khan, Masud Hussain, Ph.D., D.Litt. Javed Manzil, Dodpur, Aligarh-202 001, (Urdu linguistics).

Khan, Mohd. Ali, Prof. M.A. Department of Urdu, College of Commerce, Patna-800 004, Bihar.

Khan, N.A., M.A. Department of Arabic, Persian and Islamic Studies, Visva Bharati, Santiniketan, W.B.-731 235.

Khan, Nasrullah, M.A., M.A., B.L.Sc., Asst. Librarian Osmania University Library, Osmania University, Hyderabad-500 007, A.P. (Specialisation: manuscript preservation and Arabic Literature).

Khan, R.A., M.A., M.Phil. Department of Urdu, Centre of Regional Studies, University of Hyderabad, Hyderabad-500 134 A.P.

Khan, S.M.A., Department of Urdu, B.V.P. Janata College, Jamshedpur-831 001, Bihar.

Khan, S.A., M.A., Department of Urdu, M.M. College, Bikram, 801 104.

Khan, S.A., M.A., Department of Urdu, College of Commerce, Patna-800 001, Bihar.

Khan, Hakeem Sameeur-Rahman, Ajmal Khan Tibbiya College, Aligarh Muslim University, Aligarh-202 001, U.P.

Khan, U.M.A., M.Sc, M.Th., Faculty of Sunni Theology, Aligarh Muslim University, Aligarh-202 001, U.P.

Khan, Maulana Waheedudin, C-29, Nizamuddin West, New Delhi-110 013. (Translator of *Quran*, Writer of Islamic literature and recipient of prestigious awards).

Khatoon, Rashida, Ph.D. Department of Urdu, Mahila Maha Vidyalaya, Banaras Hindu University, Varanasi-321 005, U.P.

Koya, S.M.M., M.A. Department of History, University of Calicut, P.O. Calicut-673 635, Kerala.

Kuttasseri, M., Prof. Principal, Rouzathul Uloom Arabic College, Feroke-673 632, Kerala.

Kutty, A.V. Mohideen, Principal, M.E.S. Ponnani College, Mallappuram-676 505, Kerala.

Kutty, K.I.M., Principal, M.E.S. Kalladi College, Mannarghat, Palghat-678 582, Kerala.

Labbah, Ismail, M.Phil. Department of Arabic, University of Calicut, P.O. Calicut-673 635. Kerala.

Mahajabeen, M.A. Department of Urdu, Yuvaraja's College, Mysore-570 005, Kerala.

Mahmood, M., Ph.D. Department of Political Science, Aligarh Muslim University, Aligarh-202 001, U.P.

Majid, H., M.A., Department of Urdu, J.J. College, Arrah-802 301, Bihar.

Majeed, H.R. Abdul, Prof. C/o Muslim Hostel, Mysore-570 004, Karnataka (Persian, Urdu).

Majumdar, S.M.A., Department of Islamic History and Culture, University of Calcutta, Calcutta-700 073, W.B.

Malik, S.M., Editor, Geethurai Weekly, Lakkad Kot, Hyderabad-500 002, A.P. (Specialisation: Telugu Islamic literature).

Malik, Md., M.A. Department of Urdu, R.L.S. Yadav College, Ranchi-834 001, Bihar.

Mannan, H., M.A. Department of Urdu, College of Commerce, Patna-800 004, Bihar.

Masoodi, M.M., M.A., Department of Persian, University of Kashmir, Srinagar-190 006, J & K.

Mehraj-ud-din, Ph.D., Department of Law, University of Kashmir, Srinagar-190 006, J & K.

Mehta, S.P., M.A., Ph.D. Department of Urdu, Panjab University, Chandigarh-160 014, Punjab.

Moghni, A., Prof., Ph.D. Department of English, Patna University, Patna-800 005, Bihar.

Mohideen, K.V.V., M.A. Department of Arabic, University of Calicut, P.O. Calicut-673 635, Kerala.

Mohammed, B., M.A. C/o Anvarul Islam Arabic College, Kuniyil, Kizhuparama, Kerala.

Mohammed, K.P., Principal, Sullamussalam Arabic College, Areacode, Malappuram-673 639, Kerala.

Mohd. P. Peer, Prof. M.A., Department of History, Sadakathullah Appa College, Palayamkottai-627 002, T.N.

Mohammed, Syed, Prof. M.A., M.Litt., M.Ed., PGDES, Department of English, S.A. College, Tirunelveli-627 011, T.N.

Mohammed, U., Prof. Principal, Farook College, Feroke-673 632 Calicut, Kerala.

Mujibi, S.A., M.A. Department of Urdu, Ramgarh College, Ramgarh-829 122, Bihar.

Mursaleen, G. M.Phill. Centre of West Asian Studies, Aligarh Muslim University, Aligarh-202 001, U.P.

Murtaza, H. Gulam, Prof. Department of Arabic and Persian, Allahabad University, Allahabad-211 002, U.P.

Murtazuddin, S.M., M.A. Department of Urdu, B.S. College, Dinapur-801 503, Bihar.

Mustafa, M.M. Prof. M.A. Department of Urdu and Persian, Nalanda College, Biharsharif, Nalanda-803 101, Bihar.

Nabi, Gulam, M.A., LL.B Durji Gauhar, Kralapora, Srinagar-191 113. (Editorial Member of *Kashmiri-Kahmuri Dictionary*).

Nadvi, Abul Hasan Ali, Rector, Nadwatul Ulema, Lucknow-226 007, U.P. (Recipient of King Faisal Award).

Nadvi, Abul Irfan, *Tameer-e-Hayat*, Nadwat-ul-Ulama, Lucknow-226 007, U.P.

Nadvi, Mahmudul Azhar, Co-editor, *Tameer-e-Hayat*, Nadwat-Ul-Ulama, Lucknow-226 007, U.P.

Nadvi, Mujeebullah, Editor, *Monthly Jameatur Rashad*, Azamgarh-276 001.

Nadvi, Shahabuddin, 165, Dasarahalli, Bangalore-560 057, Karnataka.

Nadvi, Shamsh-ul-Huq, Co-editor, *Tameer-e-Hayat*, Nadwat-ul-Ulama, Lucknow-226 007, U.P.

Naimullah, M., M.A. Department of Urdu, K. Orion College, Gumla-835 207, Bihar.

Naqvi, M.S.K., Prof. Faculty of Shia Theology, Aligarh Muslim University, Aligarh-202 001, U.P.

Naqvi, S.Y.H., M.A. Department of Urdu, Doranda College, Ranchi-834 001, Bihar.

Naqvi, Z.H., M.A. Centre of West Asian Studies, Aligarh Muslim University, Aligarh-202 001, U.P.

Naqvi, Z.H., M.A. Department of Persian, Urdu and Arabic, Punjabi University, Patiala-147 002, Punjab.

Nizami, K.A., Department of History, Aligarh Muslim University, Aligarh-202 001, U.P.

Nizami, U., M.A. Department of Urdu, S.S. College, Jahanabad (Gaya)-823 001, Bihar.

Nizamuddin, Ph.D. Department of Hindi, Islamia College, Srinagar, J & K. (Hindi writer on Islam).

Nooruddin, Md., M.A. Department of Urdu, Bangalore University, Bangalore-560 005, Karnataka.

Alimunnisa Piar, M.A., Santipur, Gauhati, Assam-781 009.

Qadir, M.A., Prof. M.A. 7th Cross, Shivaji Main Road, N.R. Mohalla, Mysore-570 007, Karnataka, (Urdu).

Qadir, Syed Habeebulla (Rasheed Pasha), Rector, Jamia Nizamia, Doodh Bowli, Hyderabad-500 002, A.P.

Qadri, Syed Iqbal, M.A. Head of Department of Journalism, Maharaja's College, Mysore-570 005, Karnataka.

Qalandhar, M.S.Q., B.A. 198, Jawahar Nagar, Srinagar, J & K (or Deputy Director General, A.I.R., New Delhi-110 001) Writer in Urdu, English and Kashmiri on various topics).

Quamar, J., M.A. Department of Urdu, S.S. Memorial College, Ranchi-834 001, Bihar.

Qamar, T.A., M.A. Department of Urdu, R.S. More College, Govindpur, Bihar.

Qanungo, S.N., Prof. Ph.D. Department of History, Lucknow University, Lucknow-226 007, U.P.

Qasmi, K., Prof. M.A. Department of Urdu, Aligarh Muslim University, Aligarh-202 001, U.P.

Qasmi, M.A., M.A. Department of Islamic Studies, Aligarh Muslim University, Aligarh-202 001, U.P.

Qasmi, M. Israrul Huq, Editor, Aljamiat, 1 Bahadur Shah Zafar Marg, New Delhi-110 002.

Qasmi, Usman Ahmed, Maulvi, Fazil, Faiz-e-Jamil Library, Shahganj, Jaunpur, U.P. (Urdu writer on Islam).

Quraishi, B.H., M.A. Department of Urdu, Gulbarga University, Gulbarga-585 106, Karnataka.

Quraishi, M.A., M.A. Department of Urdu, Sheodani College, Kaler, 824 127-Gaya, Bihar.

Rahman, Anisur, Ph.D. Editor, Islam and the Modern Age, New Delhi-110 025.

Rahman, H.K.M. Fazlur, Principal, Govt. Nizamiya Tibbi College, Hyderabad-500 002, A.P.

Rahman, M.S., M.A. Department of Arabic, University of Delhi, Delhi-110 007.

Rahman, S.A., M.A. (Arabic) Centre of African and Asian Languages, Jawaharlal Nehru University, New Delhi-110 067.

Rahman, Syed, A., M.A. (Arabic) Department of Arabic, Persian and Urdu, Sri Venkateshwara University, Tirupati-517 502, A.P.

Rahman, Syed Abdul, Prof, M.A. 436, Haji Street, Vaniyambadi, T.N.-635 752, (Islamic Studies, Tamil).

Rehman, T. Abdur, Department of Economics, New College, Madras-600 014, T.N.

Rahman, Maulana Khalid Saifullah, Darululoom Sabeelussalam, 6-117, Balapur, Hyderabad-500 005, A.P., (Islamic Law).

Rahimathullah, B., Ph.D. Department of Political Science, Aligarh Muslim University, Aligarh-202 001, U.P.

Raja, H., M.A. Department of Urdu, S.S. Memorial College, Ranchi-834 001, Bihar.

Ramakrishna Rao, K.B., Prof. Department of Philosophy, University of Mysore, Mysore-570 006, Karnataka.

Rashid, Abdul M.A. Department of Urdu, T.P.S. College, Patna-800 004, Bihar.

Raza, J., Ph.D. Department of Urdu, University of Kashmir, Srinagar-190 006 J & K.

Razack, P. Abdul, M.A., B.L.Sc. Department of Arabic, University of Calicut, P.O. Calicut-673 635, Kerala.

Rizvi, A.H., M.A. Centre of West Asian Studies, Aligarh Muslim University, Aligarh-202 001, U.P.

Rizvi, K.U., M.A. Department of Arabic and Persian, University of Allahabad, Allahabad-211 002, U.P.

Rizvi, Syed Ameenul Hassan Ali, Publication Officer, Jamia Hamdard, New Delhi-110 062. (Islamic Studies/Journalist).

Rizvi, S.S.A., M.A. Department of Urdu, Giridih College, Giridih-815 301, Bihar.

Rizvi, Maulana Taher, Shaikul *Hadith*, Jamia Nizamia, Doodh Bowli, Hyderabad-500 002, A.P.

Sabir, Z.A. M.A. Department of Urdu and Persian, Nalanda College, Biharsharif, Nalanda-803 101.

Safiullah, Syed, M.A., Department of Arabic, Persian and Urdu, Oriental Research Institute, University of Madras, Madras-600 005, T.N.

Sahar, Abul Qasim, A.M., Prof. Ph.D. 39, Malviya Nagar, Bhopal-462 003, M.P.

Saiyed, A.R., Prof. Ph.D. Head, Department of Sociology, Jamia Millia Islamia, New Delhi-110 025.

Samiulla, S. Mir, M.A. Department of History, Institute of Correspondence and Continuing Education, Mysore-570 006, Karnataka.

Sargiro, S.A., M.A. Department of Persian and Urdu, Karnataka University, Dharwad-585 003, Karnataka.

Shaik, Safia, M.A. Department of Persian and Urdu, Karnataka University, Dharwad-585 003, Karnataka.

Shaharyar, A.M., Ph.D. C-13, Medical College Campus, Aligarh Muslim University, Aligarh-202 001, (Urdu).

Shekar, C., M.A. Department of Persian, University of Delhi, Delhi-110 007.

Sherwani, A.A.K., M.A. Centre of West Asian Studies, Aligarh Muslim University, Aligarh-202 001, U.P.

Shoaid, S.M., M.A. Department of Urdu, G.L.A. College, Daltonganj-822 101, Bihar.

Shoukat, Md., M.A., Department of Urdu, S.N. Sinha College, Tekari, 824 236, Bihar.

Shujat, Fatima, Prof. Ph.D. Department of Sociology, University College for Women, Koti, Hyderabad-500 001, A.P.

Siddique, A.M., M.A., Department of Urdu, J. Jain College, Jhumritalaiya-825 409, Bihar.

Siddiqi, F.M.A., Department of Islamic History and Culture, University of Calcutta Calcutta-700 073, W.B.

Siddiqi, M.Z., Ph.D. Department of Law, Aligarh Muslim University; Aligarh-202 001, U.P.

Siddiqui, Najma, Ph.D. Department of Public Administration, University College for Women, Koti, Hyderabad-500 001, A.P.

Siddiqui, S.A., M.A. Department of Urdu, S.V.P. College, Bhabua-821 101, Bihar.

Siddiqui, Z.M. Shahid, Ph.D. Faculty of Law, University of Kashmir, Srinagar-190 006, J & K.

Singh, Gulwant, M.A. Department of Persian, Urdu and Arabic, Punjabi University, Patiala-147 002, Punjab.

Sirajuddin, M.A. Department of Urdu, Gaya College, Gaya-823 001, Bihar.

Sufi, Syed A. Qader, Musahih, Dairat-ul-Maarif, Hyderabad-500 007. (Arabic language and literature, Islamic studies).

Sultana, Barjis, M.A. Department of Urdu, Manasagangotri, Mysore-570 006, Karnataka.

Sultana, Saleha, M.A. Department of Urdu, Kakatiya University, Warangal-506 009, A.P.

Saroor, Ali Ahmad, Prof. Director, Iqbal Institute, University of Kashmir, Srinagar-190 006, J & K.

Sherwani, A.A.K., M.A. Centre of West Asian Studies, Aligarh Muslim University, Aligarh-202 001, U.P.

Tayyab, H.M. Prof. Ph.D. Ajmal Khan Tibbiya College, Aligarh-202 001, U.P.

Usmani, A., M.A. Department of Urdu, Ranchi University, Ranchi-834 008, Bihar.

Usmani, Mohsin, M.A. Centre for West Asian and African Studies, Jawaharlal Nehru University, New Delhi-110 067.

Usmani, S.H., M.A. Department of Urdu, Worker's College, Jamshedpur, 813 001, Bihar.

Vajeahuddin, M.Phil. Department of Persian, M.S. University, Baroda-390 002, Gujarat.

Vijaypur, A.R., M.Phil. Department of Political Science, Aligarh Muslim University, Aligarh-202 001, U.P.

Wadood, Mufti Abdul, Naib Mufti, Darul Uloom Sabeelussalam, Balapur, Hyderabad-500 005, A.P.

Wahid A., Prof. Ph.D. Head, Department of Economics, University of Kashmir, Srinagar-190 006, J & K.

Wani, A.M., Prof., Ph.D. Department of Law, University of Kashmir, Srinagar-190 006, J & K.

Wari, R., Department of Persian, SMSG College, Sherghati-824 211, Bihar.

Waseem, M., Prof. Ph.D. Department of English, Jamia, Millia, Islamia, New Delhi-110 025.

Yunus, M.D., M.A. Department of Urdu, Ramgarh College, Ramgarh-829 122, Bihar.

Yusuf, Syed, Editor, Radiance, 2448, Baradari, Ballimaran, Sher Afghan, Delhi-110 006.

Zahid, M., M.A. Department of Urdu, Aligarh Muslim University, Aligarh-202 001, U.P.

Zaidi, S.M.K.Q. Department of Library Science, Aligarh Muslim University, Aligarh-202 001, U.P.

Ziauddin, Khaja, B.A., LL.M. 1-9-294, Vidyanagar, Hyderabad-500 044, (Specialisation: Islamic Law).

Zamarrud, H., Department of Library Science, Aligarh Muslim University, Aligarh-202, 001, U.P.

Zarina, Mumtaz, Prof., M.A. Department of Urdu, Maharaja's College, Mysore-570 005. Karnataka.

4. INSTITUTIONS

Centres of Learning Language and Literature
Colleges and Departments in Universities
Devoted to Study and Research
Libraries
Sponsoring/Funding Agencies
Publishing/Distributing Agencies

CENTRES OF LEARNING LANGUAGE AND LITERATURE

Arabic Madrasa-e-mohammadia, 5 TVK Nagar, 1st Street, Madras-600012, Tamil Nadu.

Baquiatus Salehat, Vellore-632001, Tamil Nadu.

Calcutta Madrasa, Wessley Square, Calcutta-700016, W.B.

Darul-Ulum Ahmadiya Salafiya, Laheri Asarai-846001, Bihar.

Darul-Uloom, Ahmednagar-414001, Maharashtra.

Darul Uloom Anwarul Huda, Nadi Moosaguda, Bahadurpura, Hyderabad-500264, A.P.

Darul Uloom Arabic College, Vazhakkad-673 640, Kerala.

Darul-Ulum, Baskandi, Distt. Cachar-788 001, Assam.

Darul Uloom Bhatmara, Bhalki Taluq, Distt. Bidar-585 328, Karnataka.

Darul-Ulum Chappi, Chappi, Distt. Bansakantha-385 210, Gujarat.

Darul-Uloom Deoband, Deoband, Saharanpur Distt.-247 554, U.P.

Darul Uloom Firangi Mahal, Luchnow-226 007, U.P.

Darul-Ulum Furqaniya, Tonk-340 001, Rajasthan.

Darul Uloom Hyderabad, Shivarampalli, Hyderabad-500 252, A.P.

Darul-Ulum Islamiya, Bhilai-490 001, Distt. Raipur, M.P.

Darul-Uloom, Kaurampet, Distt. Mahabubnagar-509 001, A.P.

Darul-Uloom Khanpura, Kharkhana Guda, Kareemnagar-505 001, A.P.

Darul-Ulum Khaliliya, Nizamiya, Tonk-340 001, Rajasthan.

Darul Ulum Latifi, Katihar-854 105, Bihar.

Darul-Ulum Madrasa, Ashrafiya Arabiya Islamiya, Rander, Gujarat.

Darul Uloom Moosaviya Azmatul Islam, Koka Bazar, Hussaini Alam Road, Hyderabad-500 002, A.P.

Darul Uloom, Nalgonda, Masjidgadhi, Nalgonda-508 001, A.P.

Darul-Ulum Nasiriya, Tonk-340001, Rajasthan.

Darul Uloom Rasheediya, Gadwal-509 125, Distt. Mahaboobnagar, A.P.

Darul-Ulum Rizawiya, Korba-495 677, Distt. Bilaspur, M.P.
Darul-Uloom Sabiluss Salam, 6-117, Balapur, Hyderabad-500 005, A.P.
Darul Uloom Sabeelur Rashad, (Arabic College) Bangalore-560 045, Karnataka.
Darul-Ulum Shah Alam, Ahmedabad, 380001, Gujarat.
Darul-Uloom Siddiqia, Mysore-570 015, Karnataka.
Darul-Ulum Tajul-Masjid, Bhopal, M.P.
Darus-Salam, Oomerabad-635 808, Tamil Nadu.
Jamaliya Arabic College, Madras-600001, Tamil Nadu.
Jamia Anwarul-Ulum, Tiruchinapalli-620 001, Tamil Nadu.
Jamia Arabiya Darus Salam, 16-9-406 Old Malakpet, Hyderabad-500 036. A.P.
Jamia Arabiya, Mathura-281001, U.P.
Jamia Arabia, Sevanagar, Distt. Medak-502 001, A.P.
Jamia Arabiya Bait ul Uloom, Sirpur Kagaznagar-504 296, Distt. Adilabad, A.P.
Jamia Arabiya Ihyaul-Ulum, Mubarakpur, Azamgarh-276 404, U.P.
Jamia Arabiya Islamiya, Nagpur-440001, Maharashtra.
Jamia Arabiya Madinatul Uloom, Mahaboobnagar-509 001, A.P.
Jamia Arabiya Masudiya, Bahraich-271 801, U.P.
Jamia Arabiya, Sevanagar, Patancheru, 502 324, Distt. Medak, A.P.
Jamia Arabiya Talimu-Din, Dabhel-396 415, Gujarat.
Jamia Arabiya Talimul-Islam, Anand-388 001, Gujarat.
Jamia Darul Irfan, Red Hills, Hyderabad-500 004, A.P.
Jamia Darus Salam, Delhi Gate, Malerkotla-148 023, Punjab.
Jamia Husainiya, Rander-395 005, Gujarat.
Jamia Islamiya, Bhatkal, Distt. North Kanara-581 320, Karnataka.
Jamia Islamiya Arabiya, Amroha, Distt. Moradabad-244 001, U.P.
Jamia Islamia Arabiya, Bhongir, Distt. Nalgonda-508 116, A.P.
Jamia Islamia Arabiya, Bhopal-462 001, M.P.
Jamia Islamia Madania, Bankara, Calcutta-700 051, W.B.
Jamia Latifiya, Vellore-632 001, Tamil Nadu.
Jamia Mansubia, Meerut-250 001, U.P.
Jamia Mazharul-Ulum, Varanasi, 221 001, U.P.
Jamia Miftahur-Ulum, Distt. Azamgarh-275 101, U.P.
Jamia Mohamadiya Arabic College, Rayadrug, Anantapur-515 865, A.P.
Jamiya Nizamiya, Shibli Gunj, Hyderabad-500 002, A.P.

Jamia Nizamiya, Lucknow-226 007, U.P.
Jamia Rahmaniya, Monghyr-811 201, Bihar.
Jamiya Riyadul Islam, Uppal, Hyderabad-500 039, A.P.
Jamia Qasimiya Madrasa Shahi, Moradabad-244 001, U.P.
Jamia Saifiya, Surat-395 001, Gujarat.
Jamia Tibbiya, Deoband-247 554, U.P.
Jamiat ul Banat, Saidabad Colony, Hyderabad-500 036, A.P.
Kashif ul Uloom, Jangaon, Distt. Warangal-506 002, A.P.
Madina Darul-Ulum, Akra, 24, Parganas, West Bengal.
Madinatul Uloom, Kodad-508 206, Distt. Nalgonda, A.P.
Madrasa Afsarul-Ulum, Mangalkot, Tripura.
Madrasa Ahmadiya, Faizabad-224 001, U.P.
Madrasa Ahmadiya, Arrah, Distt. Shahabad-802 301, Bihar.
Madrasa Ainul-Ilm, Shahjahanpur-242 001, U.P.
Madrasa Alhilal, Kolegal-571 440, Karnataka.
Madrasa Aliya, Fatehpuri, Delhi-110 006.
Madrasa Aliya, Rampur-224 901, U.P.
Madrasa Aliya Islamia, Chila, Amroha, Distt. Moradabad-224 001, U.P.
Madrasa Anwarul-Ulum, Gaya-823 001, Bihar.
Madrasa Anwarul-Ulum, Rajapur, Distt. Ratnagiri-415 612, Maharashtra.
Madrasa Anwarul Uloom, Vanaparti, Distt. Mahboobnagar-509 001, A.P.
Madrasa Arabiya Anwarul Uloom, Warangal-506 002, A.P.
Madrasa Arabiya Babul Uloom, Daishaipet Road, Warangal-506 002, A.P.
Madrasas Arabiya Darul Uloom, Hindupur-515 201, A.P.
Madrasa Arabiya Darul Uloom Hussainiya, Hindupur-515 201, A.P.
Madrasa Arabiya Darul Uloom Chirala, Nawabpeth, Chirala, Prakasham Distt. A.P.
Madrasa Arabiya Darul Uloom Rahmaniya, Rangeli Khidki, Yaqootpura, Hyderabad-500 023, A.P.
Madrasa Arabiya Islamiya, Nuh, Distt. Gurgaon-122 107, Haryana.
Madrasa Arabiya Islamia, Bijnathpara, Distt. Raipur-492 001, M.P.
Madrasa Arabiya Jafariya Hidayatul-Ulum, Basti-272 001, U.P.
Madrasa Arabiya Miftahul-Ulum, Bhiwandi, Distt. Thana-421 302, Maharashtra

Madrasa Arabia Misbahul Uloom, Bahmanipura, Gulbarga-585 101, Karnataka.

Madrasa Arabiya Noorul Uloom, Koheer, Dist, Medak-502 001, A.P.

Madrasa Arabiya *Quran*iya, Etawa-206 001, U.P.

Madrasa Arabiya Rauzathul Uloom Nikalvaya, Nizampeth, Distt. Medak-502 371, A.P.

Madrasa Arabiya Sirajul Uloom, Wakf Complex, Mahaboobnagar-509 001, A.P.

Madrasa Ashrafiya, Naya Bhojpur, Distt. Shahabad-802 145, Bihar.

Madrasa Atharul Uloom, Zaheerabad, Distt. Medak-502 001, A.P.

Madrasa Atharul-Muslimin, Gudur, Distt. Nellore-524 101, A.P.

Madrasa Aziziya, Bihar Sharif-803 101, Bihar.

Madrasa Azmalia Calcutta, Lower Chitpur Road, Calcutta-700 001, W.B.

Madrasa Babul Uloom, 1 Dr. Suresh Sarkar Road, Calcutta-700 014, W.B.

Madrasa Baitul Uloom Pipli Mirza, Yamunanagar Distt. Ambala-135 001, Haryana.

Madrasa Baitul Uloom, Suryapet, Distt. Nalgonda-508 213, A.P.

Madrasa-e-Burhaniya Education Society, 142, Angappa Naiken Street, Madras-600 001, Tamil Nadu.

Madrasa Chasma-i-Rahmat, Ghazipur-233 001, U.P.

Madrasa Darul Hasmath, Eidgah Ujale Shah, Saidabad, Hyderabad-500 036, A.P.

Madrasa Darul Uloom Khaleelia, Aiwan-i-shahi, Gulbarga-585 101, Karnataka.

Madrasa Darul Uloom Karimnagar, Khanpura Karkhanaguda, Kareemnagar-505 001, A.P.

Madrasa Darul Uloom Jamia Arabia, Bhainsa-504 103, Distt. Adilabad, A.P.

Madrasa Darul Uloom Mohammadia, Mohalla Bhaktapur, Distt. Adilabad-504 001, A.P.

Madrasa Deeniya Arabiya Mishkatul Uloom, Awaisi Nagar, Nizamabad-503 001, A.P.

Madrasa Diniya Islamiya, Ghazipur-233 001, U.P.

Madrasa Faiz-i-Am, Kanpur-208 001, U.P.

Madrasa Faiz-i-Am, Siwhari, Distt. Bijnor-246 701, U.P.

Madrasa Faiz-i-Am, Maunathbhanjan, Distt. Azamgarh-275 101, U.P.

Madrasa Faizul Uloom, Guntur-522 001, A.P.

Madrasa Faizul-Uloom, 16-2-837, Saidabad, Hyderabad-500 036, A.P.
Madrasa Faizul-Ulum, Seoni, Distt. Chhindwara-480 001, M.P.
Madrasa Faizul Uloom Hussainiya, Makthal, Distt. Mahaboobnagar-509 208, A.P.
Madrasa Falah-i-Darain, Tadkeshwar, Distt. Surat-394 170, Gujarat.
Madrasa Fauqaniya, Osmanabad-413 501, Maharashtra.
Madrasa Hanafiya, Gonda-271 001, U.P.
Madrasa Hanafiya, Nomaniya, Danapur, Distt. Patna-800 001, Bihar.
Madrasa Himayatul-Islam, Calicut-673 001, Kerala.
Madrasa Hufar Arabiya Taalimul Islam, Jamia Masjid Raispet, Bodhan-503 185, A.P.
Madrasa Husainiya, Sriwardhan, Distt. Kolaba, Maharashtra.
Madrasa-i-Aizza, Malakpet, Hyderabad-500 024, A.P.
Madrasa Imdadiya, Laheriasarai, Distt. Darbhanga-846 001, Bihar.
Madrasa Imdadiya, Moradabad-244 001, U.P.
Madrasa Imdadiya Darul Uloom, Beemgal, Distt. Medak-502 001, A.P.
Madrasa Imdadul-Islam, Meerut-250 001, U.P.
Madrasa Islahul-Muslimin, Patna-800 001, Bihar.
Madrasa Islamiya Arabiya, Darul-Ulum, Maunathbhanjan, Distt. Azamgarh-275 101, U.P.
Madrasa Islamiya Arabiya Baitul Uloom, Momin Mohalla, Gadwal-509 125, Distt. Mahboobnagar, A.P.
Madrasa Islamiya Arabiya Sirajul Uloom, Hashmathpet, Secunderabad-500 003, A.P.
Madrasa Islamiya Sahmsul-Huda, Patna-800 004, Bihar.
Madrasa Israil, Sarai Mir, Distt. Azamgarh-276 305, U.P.
Madrasa Jafriya, 22-8-325, Darus Shifa, Hyderabad-500 024, A.P.
Madrasa Jamiul-Ulum, Muzaffarpur-842 001, Bihar.
Madrasa Kanzul-Ulum, Tanda, Distt. Faizabad-224 190, U.P.
Madrasa Razul Uloom, Bangalore-500 026, Karnataka.
Madrasa Kausar, Aarifnagar, Shah Saheb Gutta, Mahaboobnagar-509 001, A.P.
Madrasa Madinatul-Ulum, Nagpur-440 001, Maharashtra.
Madrasa Madeenat-ul Uloom, Masjid Sarai, Miryalguda, Distt. Nalgonda-508 001, A.P.
Madrasa Manzarul-Islam, Bareilly-243 001, U.P.
Madrasa Masudiya Nurul Uloom, Bahraich-271 801, U.P.

Madrasa Mazahirul Uloom, Fertilizer City, Godavari Khani, Distt. Kareemnagar-505 001, A.P.
Madrasa Mazharul Uloom, B.H.E.L., Ramachandrapuram, Hyderabad, 500 001, A.P.
Madrasa Miftahul Uloom, Narsapur, Distt. Medak-502 001, A.P.
Madrasa Miftahul-Ulum, Jalalabad, Distt. Saharanpur-242 221, U.P.
Madrasa Minhajul Uloom, Medak-502 002, A.P.
Madrasa Mishkatul-Huda, Calicut-673 001, Kerala.
Madrasa Muhammadiya, Calicut-673 002, Kerala.
Madrasa Muhammadia, Gowdia Mutt Road, Near Music Academy, Madras-600005, Tamil Nadu.
Madrasa Muiniya, Ajmer-305 001, Rajasthan.
Madrasa-e-Niswan, Maracoir Labbai Street, Madras-600 001, Tamil Nadu.
Madrasa-e-Niswan, Vaniyambadi-635 751, Tamil Nadu.
Madrasa Nusratul Uloom, Gojranvala.
Madrasa Qasimiya Arabiya, Nagina, Distt. Bijnor-246 762, U.P.
Madrasa Qasimiya Islamiya, Gaya-823 001, Bihar.
Madrasa *Quran*iya, Jaunpur-222 001, U.P.
Madrasa Riyazul Islam, Wemapalli, Miryalguda, Distt. Nalgonda-508 001, A.P.
Madrasa Serajul Uloom, Mandi, Bazar, Warangal-506 002, A.P.
Madrasa Sirajul Uloom, Mysore Road, Chamrajpet, Near Muslim Graveyard, Bangàlore-560 002, Karnataka.
Madrasa Sulaimaniya, Patna-800 004, Bihar.
Madrasa Sultaniya, Cuttack-753 001, Orissa.
Madrasa Zeenatul *Quran*, Arabiya Collège, Chilkalooripet-522 616, Distt. Guntur, A.P.
Madrasa Ziyaul-islam, Suri-731 101, Distt. Birbhum, W. Bengal.
Madrasatul Arabia Siraj Uloom, Near Namboor Railway Station, Distt. Guntur-522 508, A.P.
Madrasatul-Islah, Khujwah, Distt. Saran-841 502, Bihar.
Madrasatul-Islam, Sarai Mir-276 305, U.P.
Madrasatul-Waizin, Lucknow-226 001, U.P.
Markazi Darul-Ulum, (Jamiatus Salafiah), BHU Campur, Riori Talab, Varanasi-221 005, U.P.
Mazahirul-Ulum, Saharanpur-247 001, U.P.
Nadvatul Ulama, P.O. Box 93, Lucknow-226 007, U.P.
Sultanul-Madaris, Lucknow-226 001, U.P.

COLLEGES AND DEPARTMENTS IN UNIVERSITIES

Aligarh Muslim University, Aligarh-202 001, U.P.

Centre of West Asian Studies.
Department of Arabic.
Department of Islamic Studies.
Department of Persian.
Department of Urdu.
Faculty of Shia Theology, Faculty of Sunni Theology.
International Council for the Study of Afro-Asian Geography.

Affiliated Colleges

Ajmal Khan Tibbia College, Aligarh, U.P.

Allahabad University, Allahabad-211 002, U.P.

Department of Arabic and Persian, Department of Urdu.

Affiliated Colleges

Unani Medical College, Allahabad, U.P.

Andhra University, Waltair-530 002, A.P.

Faculty of Oriental Learning.

Banaras Hindu University, Varanasi-221 005, U.P.

Department of Persian.
Department of Urdu.
Faculty of Oriental Learning and Theology.

Bangalore University, Bangalore-560 056, Karnataka

Department of Urdu.

Affiliated Colleges

Abbas Khan College for Women, Bangalore-560 002.
Al-Ameen College, Hosur Road, Bangalore-560 027.
Government Unani Medical College, Bangalore.
Al-Hasanath College, Dickenson Road, Bangalore-560 042

Bhagalpur University, Bhagalpur-812 007, Bihar

Department of Urdu.

Bharatidasan University

Affiliated College

Oriental College, Bharmapuram, Mayiladuthurai-609 001, Tamil Nadu.

Bihar University, Muzaffarpur-842 001, Bihar

Department of Persian.

Bhopal Vishwavidyalaya

Affiliated College

Safia College, Bhopal, M.P.

Bombay University, Bombay-400 032, Maharashtra

Department of Foreign Languages, Department of Urdu.

Affiliated Colleges

Akbar Peerbhoy College, Bombay-400 008.
Anjuman Khairul Islam Tibbia College, Bombay.
Burhani College, Mazagaon, Bombay-400 010.
Haji Rashid Jaffar College, Andheri, Bombay.
Ismail Yusuf College, Jogeshawari, Bombay-400 060.

Tibbia College, Nagpada, Bombay,

University of Calcutta, Calcutta-700 073, W.B.

Department of Urdu.
Department of Arabic and Persian.
Department of Islamic History and Culture.

Affiliated College

Maulana Azad College, Calcutta-700 013

Calicut University, Calicut University, P.O. 673 635, Kerala

Department of Arabic.

Affiliated Colleges

Aliya Arabic College, Paravanadkm, Kerala
Ansar Arabic College, Valavannur, Tirur, Mallapuram-676 555, Kerala
Anavarul Islam Arabic College, Kuniyil, Kizhuparamba, Kerala
Anvarul Islam Arabic College for Women, Kondotty, Mallapuram-673 638, Kerala
Farook College, Feroke-673 632, Calicut, Kerala
Jamia Madinatul-Ulum Arabic College, Pulikkal, Mallapuram, Kerala
MES Asmabi College, Vemmabalore, Kerala
MES Kalladi College, Mannarghat, Palghat-678 582, Kerala
MES Ponnani College, Ponnani, Mallapuram-679 577, Kerala
MES Valancherry College, Valancherry-676 552, Kerala
Madrasa Aliya Arabic College, Kasargod, Kerala
Mambad College, Mambad, Kerala
Pocker Sahib M.O. College, Thirurangadi, Mallapuram, Kerala
Rauzatul-Uloom Arabic College, Feroke, Calicut-673 632, Kerala
Sir Syed College, Taliparamba-670 141, Kerala
Sullamussalam Arabic College, Arcacode, Mallapuram-673 639, Kerala

Central Institute of English and Foreign Language,
Hyderabad-500007, A.P

Department of Arabic.

Delhi University, Delhi-110 007

Department of Arabic.
Department of Persian.
Department of Urdu.

Affiliated Colleges

Ayurved and Unani Tibbia College, Delhi-110 005.

Gorakhpur University, Gorakhpur-273 001. U.P.

Department of Urdu.

Gujarat University, Ahmedabad-380 009

Department of Persian.

Gulbarga University, Gulbarga-585 106. Karnataka

Department of Urdu and Persian.

Himachal Pradesh University

Urdu Teaching and Research Centre, Saproon, Solan-173 212, Himachal Pradesh.

University of Hyderabad, Hyderabad-500134

Department of Urdu, Centre of Regional Studies.

Jamia Hamdard, Hamdard Nagar, New Delhi-110 062

Indian Institute of Islamic Studies.

Institute of History and Research.

Affiliated Colleges

Hamdard Tibbiya College, Ballimaran, New Delhi-110 006.

Jamia Millia Islamia, Jamia Nagar, New Delhi-110 025.

Department of Islàmic and Arab Iranian Studies.
Department of Urdu.
Dr. Zakir Husain Institute of Islamic Studies.

University of Jammu, Jammu-180 001

Department of Urdu.

Jawaharlal Nehru University, New Delhi-110 067

Centre for West Asian and African Studies.
Centre of African and Asian Language.

Kanpur University

Affiliated Colleges

Halim Muslim P.G. College, Kanpur, U.P.

Kakatiya University

Affiliated Colleges

Islamia College, Warangal. A.P.

Karnataka University

Affiliated Colleges

Anjuman College, Bhatkal-581 320, Karnataka.
Anjuman College, Bijapur-586 101, Karnataka.

University of Kashmir, Srinagar-190 006

Department of Arabic.
Department of Islamic Studies.
Department of Persian.
Department of Urdu.

Affiliated Colleges

Islamia College, Srinagar-190 001, J & K
Islamia College for Women, Sopore-193 201, J & K.

Kerala University

Affiliated Colleges

Iqbal College, Peringammala, Trivendrum-675 563, Kerala.
Milad-e-Shariff Memorial College, Kayamkulam-690 502, Kerala.

L.N. Mithila University Darbhanga-846 004, Bihar

Department of Urdu.

Lucknow University, Lucknow-226 007, U.P.

Department of Arabic.
Department of Persian.
Department of Urdu.

Affiliated Colleges

Mumtaz College, Lucknow-226 001, U.P.
Takmil-ut-Ṭibb College, Lucknow-226 001, U.P

University of Madras, Madras-600 005, Tamil Nadu

Department of Arabic, Persian and Urdu.

Affiliated Colleges

C. Abdul Hakeem College, Melvisharam-632 509, Tamil Nadu
Govt. College of Indian System and Medicine, (Unani Branch) Madras-600 106, Tamil Nadu
Islamia College, Vaniyambadi-635 751, Tamil Nadu
Jamal Mohamed College, Tiruchinapalli-620 020, Tamil Nadu
Justice Basheer Ahmed Sayed College for Woman, Teynampet, Madras-600 018
Khader Mohideen College, Adirampattinam-614 701, Tamil Nadu
Mazharul Uloom College, Ambur, North Arcot-635 802, Tamil Nadu
New College, Madras-600 014, Tamil Nadu
Quaide Millat College for Men, Medavakka, Madras-600 042, Tamil Nadu
Quaide-Millat Govt. College for Women, Madras-600 042, Tamil Nadu

Madurai Kamraj University

Affiliated Colleges

Hajee Karutha Rawthar Howdia College, Uthamapalayam-635 751, Tamil Nadu
Sadakathulla Appa College, Palayamkottai-627 002, Tamil Nadu
Wakf Board College, Madurai, Tamil Nadu.

Magadh University, Bodh Gaya-824 234, Bihar

Department of Urdu.

Affiliated Colleges

Al Hafiz College, Arrah-802301, Bihar.
Allama Iqbal College, Bihar Shareef, Nalanda-803 101, Bihar.
Mirza Ghalib College, Gaya-823 001, Bihar.

Meerut University

Affiliated Colleges

Ismail National Degree College for Women, Meerut, U.P.

Mysore University, Manasagangothri, Mysore-570 006, Karnataka

Department of Middle Eastern Studies.
Department of Urdu.

Affiliated Colleges

Farooqia College, Eidgah, Mysore-570 015. Karnataka.
Govt. Unani Medical College, Sayyaji Road, Mysore-570 001, Karnataka.

Marathwada University

Affiliated Colleges

Maulana Azad College, Aurangabad-431 001, Maharashtra

Nagarjuna University

Affiliated Colleges

Andhra Muslim College, Puthaivari, Thata, Guntur-522 001, A.P.

University of Nagpur

Affiliated Institute

Department of Arabic, Institute of Arts and Social Sciences, Nagpur. Maharashtra.

Osmania University, Hyderabad-500 007, A.P.

Department of Arabic.
Department of Islamic Studies.
Department of Persian.
Department of Urdu.

Affiliated Colleges

A.K.M. Oriented College, Kachiguda, Hyderabad-500 027.

Anwar Ul-Uloom College, Mallepally, Hyderabad-500 001.
Govt. Nizamia Tibbi College, Hyderabad-500 002.
Latifia Arabic College, Moghul Pura, Hyderabad.
Mumtaz College, Hyderabad-500 036.
Urdu Arts Evening College, Hyderabad-500 029.

Panjab University, Chandigarh-160 014.

Department of Urdu.

Patna University, Patna-800 005, Bihar.

Department of Arabic.
Department of Persian.
Department of Urdu.

Affiliated Colleges

Govt. Tibbia College, Patna, 800 001, Bihar.
Oriental College, Patna-800 001, Bihar.

Poona University

Affiliated Colleges

Deccan College Research Institute, Pune-411 006, Maharashtra.
Mohammadiya Tibbi College, Malegaon-423 203, Maharashtra.
Poona College, Pune-411 001, Maharashtra.
Unani Medical College, Pune-411 001, Maharashtra.

Panjabi University, Patiala-147 002, Punjab

Department of Persian, Urdu and Arabic.
Department of Religious Studies.

Affiliated Institute

Government Institute of Oriental and Modern Languages, Patiala-147 001, Punjab

Rajasthan University, Jaipur-302 004, Rajasthan

Department of Urdu.

Affiliated Colleges

Rajasthan Tibbiya College, Jaipur-302 001, Rajasthan.
Rajputana Unani Tibbia College, Jaipur-302 001, Rajasthan.
Zubediya Unani College, Jodhpur-342 001, Rajasthan.

Ranchi University, Ranchi-834 008, Bihar.

Department of Urdu.

Affiliated Colleges

Abdul Bari Memorial College, Jamshedpur-831 001, Bihar.
Maulana Azad College, Ranchi-834 001, Bihar.

University of Saugar

Affiliated Colleges

Saifiya Hamidiya Unani Tibbi College, Burhanpur-450 331, M.P.

Sri Venkateshwara University, Tirupati-517 502, A.P.

Department of Arabic, Persian and Urdu Oriental Research Institute.

Affiliated Colleges

Jamia Mohammadiya Arabic College, Rayadrug, A.P.
Islamia Arabic and Tibbi College, Kurnool-518 001, A.P.
Osmania College, Kurnool-518 001. A.P.

Sukhadia University, Udaipur-313 001, Rajasthan.

Department of Urdu.

PRIVATE BODIES DEVOTED TO STUDY AND RESEARCH

Abul Kalam Azad Oriental Research Institute, Bagh-e-Aam, Hyderabad-500 001, A.P.

Abdul Bari Academi, Farangi Mahal, Lucknow-226 001, U.P.

Academy of Islamic Research and Publication, P.O. Box 93, Lucknow-226 007, U.P.

All India Council for Muslim Economic Upliftment, 179, Vazir Building, I.R. Road, Bombay-400 003, Maharashtra.

Anjuman-i-Himayat-e-Islam, Madras-600 017, T.N.

Anjuman-i-Islam Urdu Research Institute, 92, D.N. Road, Bombay-400 001, Maharashtra.

Bhandarkar Oriental Research Institute, Poona-411 004, Maharashtra.

Bureau for Promotion of Urdu (Tareqqi-i-Urdu Board), West Block-8, R.K. Puram, New Delhi-110 022.

Centre for Asian Documentation, K-15, CIT Buildings, Christopher Road, P.O. Box 11215, Calcutta-700 014, W.B.

Centre for Education and Documentation, 3 Suleman Chambers, 4 Battery Street, Bombay-400 039, Maharashtra.

Dairat-ul-Maarif al-Osmania, Osmania University Campus, Hyderabad-500 007, A.P.

Darul-*Hadith*, Badarpur, Distt. Cachar-788 806, Assam.

Darul-Musannifin, Azamgarh-276 001, U.P.

Ghalib Academy, Huzrath Nizamuddin, Delhi-110 013

Al Hilal Education Society, Bangalore Road, Chickbalapur-562 101, Karnataka.

Hyderabad Educational Conference, 19, Bachelor's Quarters, Jawaharlal Nehru Road, Hyderabad-500 002, A.P.

Idaara-e-Adabiyat-e-Urdu, Khairtabad, Hyderabad-500 004, A.P.

Idara Talimi-o-Taraqqi, Jamia Milia Islamia, New Delhi-110025.

Imam-e-Zamana Mission, 3-6-22, Himayathnagar, Hyderabad-500 029, A.P.

Imama-e-Zamana Education Society, 22-4-403, Noor Khan Bazar, Hyderabad-500 024, A.P.

Imam-Ul-Uloom Education Society, 17-9-166, Kurmaguda, Hyderabad-500 036, A.P.

Indian Society for Afro Asian Studies, 75, Defence Enclave, Vikas Marg, New Delhi-110 092.

Institute of Asian Studies, 3-4-877, Barkatpura, Hyderabad-500 027. A.P.

Institute of Islamic Studies, 2nd Floor, 4th Road, Irene Cottage, Santacruz (East) Bombay-400 055, Maharashtra.

Institute of Objective Studies, Baitul Hamid, Muradi Road, Batla House, New Delhi-110 025.

Institute of Oriental Philosophy, Vrindavan-281 121, U.P.

Iqbal Academy, Madina Mansion, Narayanguda, Hyderabad-500 029, A.P.

Iqbal Institute, Srinagar-190 006, J & K.

Iran League, Navasari Building, 2nd Floor, D.N. Road, Fort, Bombay-400 001, Maharashtra.

Iran Society, 12, Dr. M. Ishagur Road, Calcutta-700 016, W.B.

Islam and Modern Age Society, Jamia Nagar, New Delhi-110 025.

Islamia Mission, Lucknow-226 003, U.P.

Islamic Culture Board, P.B. 171, Hyderabad-500 007, A.P.

Islamic Centre, Nizamuddin West, New Delhi-110013.

Islamic Centre for Indian Minorities Studies, Madina Mansion, Narayanguda, Hyderabad-500 029, A.P.

Islamic Centre of Students and Youth, Kanakachery, Kerala.

Islamic Law Academy, Humayun Nagar, Hyderabad-500 028, A.P.

Islamic Research Association, 8 Shephard Road, Bombay-400 008, Maharashtra.

Islamic Social Service Society, 22-7-499, Purani Haveli, Hyderabad-500 002, A.P.

Islamic Society of India, 182, Netaji Road, Madras-600 001, T.N.

J.D.T. Islam, Calicut-673 012, Kerala.

K.R. Cama Oriental Institute, Apollo Street, Fort, Bombay-400 032, Maharashtra.

Khawateen-e-Deccan Library and Research Institute, Katalmandi, Hyderabad-500 001, A.P.

Majlis-e-Ilmia Andhra Pradesh, Mahboob Bazar, Chaderghat, Hyderabad-500 024, A.P.

Majlis Ishaat-e-Islam, C/o Meraj Builders, King Kothi Road, Hyderabad-500 001, A.P.

Muslim Education Society, Dandeli-581 325, Karnataka.

Muslim Educational Association of South India, 87, Peters Road, Madras-600 014, T.N.

Muslim Educational Society, 5, Prof. Subramanian Street, Madras-600 010, T.N.
Muslim Progressive Society, 21, Rapon Street, Calcutta-700 016, W.B.
Muslim Welfare Society, 98 Rabindra Saranee, Calcutta-700 001, W.B.
Muslim Women Relief and Rehabilitation Committee, 2 Shariffa Lane, Calcutta-700 016. W.B.
Muslims Women Associations, 3 Cannon Smith Road, Madras-600 006, T.N.
Naimat's Science Academy, C/o Dr. Syed Khalifathullah, Pycrofts Road, Madras-600 005, T.N.
Oriental Institute, Lokmanya Tilak Road, Baroda-390 001, Gujarat.
Oriental Institute of Indian Language, 32, Korsheed Building, P.M. Road, Bombay-400 001, Maharashtra.
Oriental Research Institute, Yelwal Road, Mysore-560 005, Karnataka.
Rajasthan Oriental Research Institute, Tonk-340 001, Rajasthan.
Shibli Academy, Azamgarh-276 001, U.P.
S.I.E.T. Islamic Trust, J.B.A.S. College for Women, Teynampet, Madras-600 018 T.N.
Sayeedia Academy, C/o Dr. Noorullah Basha, Qaida-e-Millat Road, Near Shifa Clinic, Madras-600 005, T.N.
Tippu Sultan Research Academy, Srirangapatnam-571 438, Karnataka.
Urdu Academy, 11-4-637, A.C. Guards, Hyderabad-500 004, A.P.
Urdu Ghar, Moghalpura, Hyderabad-500 002, A.P.

LIBRARIES

Government Libraries

A.P. State Archives, Hyderabad-500 007, A.P.
Amirud-Daula Govt. Public Library, Kaiser Bagh, Lucknow-226 001, U.P.
Anjuman-i-Ittehad-ul Islam Library, Sawday Road, Mysore-570 001, Karnataka.
Asafiya State Central Library, Afzal Gunj, Hyderabad-500 001, A.P.
Asiatic Society of Bombay, Town Hall, Bombay-400 001, Maharashtra.

Asiatic Society, 1 Park Street, Calcutta-700 016, W.B.
Barahne Shah Dargah Library, New Santosh Nagar, Hyderabad-500 659, A.P.
Bartala Muslim Library and Reading Room, Bartala-700 018, W.B.
Connemara Public Library, Madras-600 008, T.N.
Fatehpuri Public Library and Reading Room, Fatehpuri Mosque, Delhi-110 006.
Govt. Oriental Manuscript Library, Opp: Chadarghat High School, Abids, Hyderabad-500 001, A.P.
Govt. Oriental Manuscript Library, University Building, Madras-600 005, T.N.
Hamidia State Library, Sultanic Road, Bhopal-462 001, M.P.
Khuda Bakhsh Oriental Public Library, Patna-800 004, Bihar.
National Archives of India, Janpath, New Delhi-110 001.
National Library, Belvedere, Calcutta-700 027, W.B.
Rampur Raja Library, Rampur-244 901, U.P.
Salar Jung Museum Library, Afzal Gunj, Hyderabad-500 001, A.P.
Saulat Public Library, Rampur-244 901, U.P.

University Libraries

Allahabad University Library, Allahabad-211 002, U.P.
Bombay University Library, University Road, Bombay-400 032, Maharashtra.
C.I.E.F.L. Library, O.U. Campus, Hyderabad-500 007, A.P.
University of Calcutta Library, Calcutta-700 073, W.B.
University of Delhi Library, Delhi-110 007.
Jamia Millia Islamia Library, Jamia Nagar, New Delhi-110 025.
University of Jammu Library, Canal Road, Jammu (Tawi)-180 001, J & K.
Jawaharlal Nehru University Library, New Mehrauli Road, New Delhi-110 067.
University of Kashmir Library, Srinagar-190 006, J & K.
Lucknow University Library, Lucknow-226 007. U.P.
Maulana Azad Library, Aligarh Muslim University, Aligarh-202 001, U.P.
Mysore University Library, Manasagangotra, Mysore-570 006, Karnataka.
Osmania University Library, Hyderabad-500 007, A.P.

Punjab University Library, Chandigarh-160 014, Punjab.
Punjabi University Library, Patiala-147 002, Punjab.

Private Libraries

Central Muslim Association Library, Arcot Srinivasachar Street, Banglore-560 002, Karnataka.
Darul Mutaleatual Burhania Library, Delhiwala Building, Outside Hathipole Udaipur-313 001, Rajasthan.
H.E.H. Nizam Trust Library, 12-1-585, Syed Ali Guda, Hyderabad-500 002, A.P.
Haidari Circulating Library, Nizam Shahi Road, Hyderabad-500 001, A.P.
Hamdard Library, 14, O.B. Khadki, Pune-411 003, Maharashtra.
Henry Martin Institute of Islamic Studies, Nampally Station Road, Hyderabad-500 001, A.P.
Dr. Iqbal Library Iqbal Road, Bansmandi, Kanpur-208 001, U.P.
Islamia Library, 38, Machhua Bazar Street, Calcutta-700 007, W.B.
Islamic Information Centre, Nalband Pora, Srinagar, J & K.
Islamic Library, Shamshad Market, Aligarh-202 001, U.P.
Jalsai Tahzib Library, Rifah-e-am Building, Gulaganz, Lucknow-226 001, U.P.
Jamia Masjid Library, 46, Jankinagar Street, Bombay-400 002, Maharashtra.
Kutub Khana-i-Saidiya, Jambagh, Hyderabad.
Kutubkhana-i-Nasiriya, Lucknow-226 001, U.P.
Mahmoodia Library, C/o Masjid Abdulnabi, Shah Zafar Marg, New Delhi-110 001.
Maktaba Al-Jamaitus Saifiyah, Arabic Academy Campus, P.O. Box 336, Devdi, Surat-395 001, Gujarat.
Maktaba Gulfishan, Qazipur Kurd, Gorakhpur-273 001, U.P.
Masjid-i-Amira Library, Abids, Hyderabad-500 001, A.P.
Maulana Abul Kalam Azad Library and Reading Room, Tellicherry-670 101, Kerala.
Maulana Azad Central Library, Old Museum Building, Bhopal-462 001, M.P.
Mecca Masjid Library, Mecca Masjid, Hyderabad-500 002, A.P.
Mohammad Ali library, 6A, Kanai Seal Street, Calcutta-700 001, W.B.

Mohammedan Oriental Library, Wallaja Road, Opp. Kalaivanaarangam, Madras-600 005, T.N.
Muhammadi Library, Ramaswamy Chetty Street, Madras-600 012, T.N.
Mujahid Centre, Opp. Calicut Railway Station, Calicut-673 001, Kerala.
Muslim Library, Veerapillai Street, Bangalore-560 001, Karnataka.
Mustafa Khidmat Khalque Library, Vill. Lauwan, P.O. Haridiya, Siwan-841 232, Bihar.
Peer Mohammad Shah Dargah Library, Ahmedabad-380 001, Gujarat.
Sadar Muslim Library, Sadar Bazar, Nagpur-440 001, Maharashtra.
Seethakathi Islamic Trust Library, Near Anand Theatre, Anna Road, Madras-600 002, T.N.
Shah Siraj Library, C/o Dr. Yusuf Usman, Ajanta Clinic, Aurangabad-431 001, Maharashtra.
Shia Library, Jaunpur-222 001, U.P.
Theosophical Society, Bombay-400 007, Maharashtra.
Theosophical Society, Adyar, Madras-600 002, T.N.
Urdu Hall Library, Himayatnagar, Hyderabad-500 029, A.P.
Urdu Kutub Khana, Motihari, Distt. Champaran-845 401, Bihar.
Vidyajyothi Institute of Islamic Studies, 23, Raj Niwas Marg, Delhi-110 054.

SPONSORING/FUNDING AGENCIES

A.N. Sinha Institute of Social Studies, Patna-800 001, Bihar.
All India Council for Muslim Economic Upliftment, 179, Vazir Bldg. 1st Floor, Bombay-400 003, Maharashtra.
All India Muslim Educational Conference, Sultan Jahan Manzil, Aligarh-202 001, U.P.
Asiatic Society, 1 Park Street, Calcutta-700 016, W.B.
Azeema Hafez Educational Society, Sangareddy, Medak-502 001, A.P.
Central Wakf Council, Jam Nagar House, New Delhi-110 025.
Deeni Madrasa Board, Department of Education, Patna-800 001, Bihar.
Deeni Madrasa Board of West Bengal, Writers Building, Calcutta-700 001, W.B.

Gujarat Muslim Education Promoting Society, 684, Hazie Qureshi Marg, Mirzapur, Ahmedabad-380 001, Gujarat.

H.E.H. Nizam's Trust, 6-1-62, Opp. L.B. Stadium, Hyderabad-500 001, A.P.

Haji Md. Jan Literary Trust, 97, Coral Merchant Street, Madras-600 001, T.N.

Hamdard Education Society, Hamdard Nagar, New Delhi-110 062.

Indian Council of Historical Research, 35, Ferozshah Road, New Delhi-110 001.

Indian Council for Cultural Relations, Azad Bhawan, Indraprastha Estate, New Delhi-110 002.

Indian Council for Social Science Research, 35, Ferozshah Road, New Delhi-110 001.

Indian Council of World Affairs, Sapru House, Barakhamba Road, New Delhi-110 001.

Indian Institute of Islamic Studies, Tughluqabad, New Delhi-110 062.

India International Centre, 40, Lodi Estate, New Delhi-110 001.

Institute of Asian Studies, 3-4-877, Barkatpura, Hyderabad-500 027, A.P.

Institute of Islamic Studies, 2nd Floor, 4th Road, Irene Cottage, Santacruz (East) Bombay-400 055, Maharashtra.

Institute of Indo-Middle East Cultural Studies, Troop Bazar, Hyderabad-500 001, A.P.

Institute of Muslim Ummah Affairs, P.O. Box 77, Aligarh-202 001, U.P.

Institute of Objective Studies, Muradi Road, Batla House, New Delhi-110 025.

Islamic Academy of History of India, 10-3-68/1 Humayun Nagar, Hyderabad-500 028, A.P.

Islamic Foundation Trust, 78, Perambur High Road, Madras-600 012, T.N.

Khuda Bakhsh Oriental Public Library, Patna-800 004, Bihar.

M.A. Namazie Endowment (Public Wakf) 148, Angappa Naicken Street, Madras-600 001, T.N.

Mecca Masjid Endowment, 170, Anna Salai, Madras 600 002, T.N.

Muslim Association for Advancement of Science, Faridi House, Sir Syed Nagar, Aligarh-202 001, U.P.

Muslim Institute, 21 A, Wellesly Sq. Calcutta-700 016, W.B.

Nahjul Balagah Society, 4-1-827/3, J.N. Road, Hyderabad-500 001, A.P.

National Social Science, Documentation on Centre, 35, Feroz Shah Road, New Delhi-110 001.

Nehru Memorial Museum and Library, New Delhi-110 011.

Organization of Muslim Educational Institutions and Associations (OMEIAT) Siddique Sarai, P.H. Road, Madras-600 013, T.N.

Sahitya Akademy, Rabindra Bhawan, New Delhi-110 001.

Taraqq-i-Urdu Board, (Bureau for Promotion of Urdu) West Block-8, R.K. Puram, New Delhi-110 022.

Unity Education Trust, Hassan Saheb Compound, Kodialbel, Mangalore-575 003, Karnataka.

University Grants Commission, Bahadur Shah Zafar Marg, New Delhi-110 002.

PUBLISHING/DISTRIBUTING AGENCIES

Non-Commercial Agencies

Academy of Islamic Research and Publications, Nadwat al Ulama, Lucknow-226 007, U.P.

Academy of Islamic Studies, 470, Agapura, Hyderabad-500 002, A.P.

Anjuman Farooqia, Ibrahimpur, Post Deo Kali Tarn, Distt. Azamgarh, U.P.

Anjuman Taraqqi Urdu, Booksellers and Publishers, M.U. Market, Aligarh, U.P.

Anjuman Taraqqi-i-Urdu, Delhi-110 006.

A.P. State Archives, Hyderabad-500 007.

Arabic and Persian Research Institute (Rajasthan Oriental Research Institute), Tonk- 340 001, Rajasthan.

Asian Publications, Theatre Communication Building, Connaught Circus, New Delhi-110 001.

Asiatic Society, Park Street, Calcutta-700 016.

Asma Publications, Sharib House, Jhalra, Ajmer-305 001, Rajasthan.

Bureau for Promotion for Urdu, (Taraqqi-i-Urdu Board), West Block, 8, R.K. Puram, New Delhi-110 022.

Cincinnati Art Museum, Eden Park, Cincinnati, OH 45202, U.S.A.

Cutchi Menon Jamat of Andhra Pradesh, Secunderabad-500 003.

Crescent Publication Co., 2034, Qasimjan Street, Ballimaran, Delhi 110 006.

Dairat ul Maarif, Osmania University Campus, Hyderabad-500 007, A.P.

M.A. Dalvi Waqf, 249, Ghorpade Peth, Pune-411 042, Maharashtra.

Darul Mussanifeen, Azamgarh-276 001, U.P.

Darul Ishaat Islamiya, 18, Culcutola Street, Calcutta-700 001, West Bengal.

Al-Darussalafiah, 6/8 A Hazrat Terrace Annexe, Shaik Hafizuddin Road, Byculla, Bombay 400 008, Maharashtra.

Deen-Va-Danish Publications, Azeem Abad Colony, Patna-800 006, Bihar.

Delhi School of Social Work, University of Delhi, Delhi-110 007.

Al Fassy Publications, 151, Angappa Naicken Street, P.B. 1750, Madras-600 001.

Fazil Academy, Panj-e-Shah, Hyderabad-500 002, A.P.

Furqania Academy Trust, 165, Dasarahalli, Bangalore-560 057, Karnataka.

Ghalib Academy, Nizamuddin, New Delhi-110 013.

Hamdard (Wakf) Laboratories, Hamdard Marg, Lalkuan, Delhi-110 006.

Al Hassan Book Centre, P.B. 610, Bangalore-560 006, Karnataka.

Hyderabad Historical Society, P.O. 1771, Cambridge, MA 02238, U.S.A.

Hindustani Talimi Sangh, Sewa Gram, Wardha, Maharashtra.

I.G. Publications, 20-7-10, Shah Gunj, Hyderabad-500 002, A.P.

I.N.S.A. (Indian National Science Academy), Bahadurshah Zafar Marg, New Delhi-110 001.

Idara Dawat al *Quran*, 59, M.A. Road, Bombay-400 003, Maharashtra.

Indian Association for Afro-Asian Solidarity, 14-B, Janpath Barracks, New Delhi-110 001.

Indian Council of Social Science Research, Southern Regional Centre, Hyderabad-500 007.

Indian Institute of Advanced Study, Rashtrapathi Nivas, Simla-5.

Information Research Academy, Syed Amir Ali Avenue, P.B. 10250, Calcutta-700 019.

Institute of Indo-Middle East Cultural Studies, Troop Bazar, Hyderabad- 500 001.

Institute of Kongu Studies, Salem-636 006, T.N.

Inter-University Board of India, rose Avenue, New Delhi-110 009.

Islamic Academy of Sciences, 16-8-933/1/4/1, Hyderabad-500 036.

Islamic Culture Board, Hyderabad-500 007.

Islamic Sahitya Sadan, Ramnagar, Varanasi, U.P.

Islamic Foundation, 223, London Road, Leicester LE 21ZE, U.K.

Islamic Foundation Trust, Perambur High Road, Madras-600 012, T.N.

Jamia Darul Irfan, Red Hills, Hyderabad-500 004, A.P.

Khuda Bukhsh Oriental Public Library, Patna-800 004, Bihar.

Khwaja -Publishers, sharib House, 172, Jhabra Ajmer-305 001, Rajasthan.

Al-Kitab, Publishers and Distributors, Mayur Kushal, Gunfoundry, Hyderabad-500 001, A.P.

Kutab Khana Anjuman-e-Taraqqi-e-Urdu, Urdu Bazar, Jamia Masjid, Delhi-110 006

Markazi Maktaba Islami, 1353, Chitli Qabr, Delhi-110 006.

Maktaba Burhan, Urdu Bazar, Delhi-110 006.

Maktaba-al-faiz, Madrasa Karamatiya, Darul Faiz, Jalalapur, Faizabad-224 149, U.P.

Maktaba Jamat-e-Islami, Aminuddaula Park, Lucknow-226 001, U.P.

Maktaba Jamat-e-Islami, Chatta Bazar, Hyderabad-500 002, A.P.

Maktaba Jamat-e-Islami, Booksellers, Mohd, Ali Road, Mominpura, Nagpur-440 002, Maharashtra.

Maktaba Jamia, Jamia Nagar, New Delhi-110 025.

Maktaba Zikra, Rampur-244 901, U.P.

Ministry of Information and Broadcasting, Publications Division, New Delhi-110 001.

Al-Momin Majlis, 199/13, Das Compound, Basvanagudi, Bangalore-560 004, Karnataka.

Muhammad Taahaa Pub. Thaika Colony, Rahmath Nagar, Tirunelveli-627 011, Tamil Nadu.

Nadwat Book Agency, Iram Cottage, Azampura, Hyderabad-500 001, A.P.

National Information and Welfare Trust, Nizamuddin West, New Delhi-110 013.

National Museum, Janpath, New Delhi 110 001.

Orient Press International, New Urdu Press Service, 84, Abul Fazl Enclave, Jamia Nagar, New Delhi-110 025.

Shanti Prakashan Hidayath Centre, Bibi Allabi Road, Mangalore-575 001, Karnataka.

Al-Siddique's Islamic Book Centre, Jamia Complex, N.R. Road, Bangalore-560 002, Karnataka.

The Superintendent, Publications Division, A.M.U. Aligarh-202 002, U.P.

Unity Education Trust, Mangalore-575 003, Karnataka.

Usmani Moini G.S. Khankah, Jhalra, Ajmer-305 001, Rajasthan.

M.S. Vawda, 66, Canning Street, Calcutta-700 001.

Commercial Agencies

Aakif Book Depot, 437, Motia Mahal, Delhi-110 006.

Abdul Bakhi Bukhari Book Depot, 1912, Blundel Road, Pune-411 001, Maharashtra.

Abdul Rahim Book Sellers, Chowk, Aurangabad, 431 001, Maharashtra.

Abdul Salam Book Sellers, 12, Zakaria Street, Calcutta-799 001, W.B.

Ahmed Kunhi K.P. and Sons, Book Sellers, Camp Bazar, Cannanore-670 001, Kerala.

A.M. Ahmed and Co., Booksellers, 255, Linghi Chetty Street, Madras-600 001, T.N.

Ali Noor Saudagar Booksellers, Bari Masjid, Daltongunj-822 101, Bihar.

Amina Book Stall, Publishers and Booksellers, Post Office Road, Trichur-680 001, Kerala.

Ansari Book Depot, Huzoor Road, Calicut-673 001, Kerala.

Azeez Stores, Booksellers, Chandni Chowk, Bangalore-560 001, Karnataka.

Bilal Press, Publishers and Booksellers, Tirunelveli-627 006, T.N.

Commercial Book House, Charminar, Hyderabad-500 002, A.P.

Darul Kitab al-Islami, Ibrahimpur, Azamgarh-276 001, U.P.

Dini Kutub Khana, Kumbarpet Mosque, Bangalore-560 002, Karnataka.

Feroze Book Depot, 12 City Market, Bangalore-560 002, Karnataka.

Gulistan Book Depot, Sawday Road, Mandi Mohalla, Mysore-570 001, Karnataka.

Gujarat Book Depot, Mohalla Qilla, Deoband-247 554, U.P.

Haji M.A. Shahul Hameed and Sons, 20 High Road, Triplicane, Madras-600 005, T.N.

Haji A. Qayyum, (Haji Md. Mohsin), 15 Wesley Square, Calcutta-700 016, W.B.

Haji Mohd. Sayeed, R.A. Qidwai Road, Calcutta-700 016, W.B.

Hamdard Book Depot, Islamia High School Road, Srinagar-190 010, J & K.

Haziq and Mohi, 20-4-819, Chowk, Hyderabad-500 002, A.P.

Al Hilal Book Depot, Turab Ali Street, Mandi Mohalla, Mysore-570 001, Karnataka.

Hindustan Publication, 81, Angappa Naichen Street, Madras-600 001, T.N.

Al Huda Book Stall, Masjid Bazar, Calicut-673 001, Kerala.

Husaini Book Depot, Machli Kaman, Hyderabad-500 002, A.P.

Hussami Book Depot, Charkaman, Hyderabad-500 002, A.P.

Hyderi Prakashan, 910 Budhwar Peth, Pune-411 002, Maharashtra.

Idara-i-Adabiyat-i-Delhi, 2009, Qasimjan Street, Delhi-110 006.

Idara-i-Ishaat-e-Diniyat, Inside Zaki Hotel, Hazrat Nizamuddin, New Delhi-110 013.

Iqbal Book Depot, 5-7-557, Nampally Bazar, Hyderabad-500 001, A.P.

Islami Book Depot, Nakhasa Bazar, Saharanpur, 247 001, U.P.

Islamia Book Depot, Talak Mahal, Kanpur, 208 001, U.P.

Islamia Library, Booksellers, Barpeta, Assam-781 315.

Islamiah Book Depot, Kurnool, 518 001, A.P.

Islamic Book Centre, 20-6-550, S.A. Chabutra, Hyderabad-500 002, A. P.

Islamic Book Trust, 1397, Pahari Imli, Jama Masjid, Delhi-110 006

Islamic Book Service, 2241/32, Kucha Chalan, Daryagunj, New Delhi-110 002.

Itfal Book Depot, (Maktabe Itfal) New ward Malegaon-413 115, Maharashtra.

M.A. Jameel, Booksellers, 15A, No. 2 Street, Tasker Towri, Bangalore-560 001, Karnataka.

Kaleem Book Depot, Khas Bazar, Ahmedabad-380 001, Gujarat.

Kazmi Book Depot, New Bazar, Kirkee, Pune-411 003, Maharashtra.

Kausar Book Agency, Chatta Bazar, Hyderabad, 500 002, A.P.

Khadria Book Depot, Mominpura, Gulbarga-585 104, Karnataka

Khadria Book Depot, B.N. Street, Durrani Mosque, Mandi Mohalla, Mysore-570 001, Karnataka.

Khan Zaman Khan, Adil Manzil, Nawabs Fort, Saharanpur-247 001, U.P.

Khwaja Book Depot, D.P. Road, Panaji, 403 001, Goa.

Kitab Bhawan, 1784, Kalan Mahal, New Delhi-110 002.

Kitab Ghar, Chowk Road, Udipi Distt. South Kanara, Karnataka.

Kutub Khana Ishaat-e-Islam, 3755, Churiwalan, Delhi-110 006.

Madina Book Depot, Urdu Bazar, Jama Masjid, Delhi-110 006.

Maktaba Deeniyat, Asaf Ali Road, New Delhi-110 001.

Maktaba-e-Islam, 41, Gwynne, Lucknow, 226 001, U.P.

Maktaba-e-Islam, 172/54, Md. Ali Lane, Goen Road, Lucknow-226 018, U.P.

Maktaba Ilmiya, Qazi Street, Meerut, 250 001, U.P.

Maktaba Jamia, Aminabad, Lucknow-226 001, U.P.

Maktaba Sadaqat, Mubarakpur, Azamgarh-277 404, U.P.

Maktaba Adbi Markaz, Jadeed Road, Baramulla, Kashmir-193 101, J & K.

Malabar Islam Book Depot, Mattanchery, Cochin-682 002, Kerala.

Mansell, Artillery House, Artillery Row, London-SWIP IRT, U.K.
S.S. Mohammed Booksellers, Alangudi, Tiruchirapalli, Tamil Nadu.
Mohammed Abdul Ghani, Booksellers, Nizamabad, 503 001, A.P.
Mohamed Ali Library, Genai Sale Street, Calcutta-700 001, W.B.
Muhammadiya Pustakalaya, Dhubri, Assam-783 301.
Mulla Ismailji Kurban Hussainji, Clock Tower, Udaipur, 313 001, Rajasthan.
Muslim Book Depot, 31, City Market, Bangalore-560 002, Karnataka.
Naseem Book Depot, P.O. Kadiri, Distt. Anantapur, 515 592, A.P.
Nooruddin Ali Bhai, Booksellers, Main Road, Adilabad-504 001, A.P.
Prathiba Books, Islamic Youth Centre, Bank Road, Calicut-673 001, Kerala.
Al-Qalam Pub., 16-2-1, Saidabad, Hyderabad-500 659, A.P.
Rashid Book Depot, Mandir Bazar, Burhanpur, 450 331, M.P.
J.J. Sant Singh and Sons, Churiwalan, Delhi-110 006.
M.A. Sattar, Booksellers, Azam Gunj, Bidar, Karnataka.
Sayeedi Book Depot, Bhindi Bazar, Bombay-400 003, Maharashtra.
Shabeer Brothers, Booksellers and Publishers, Bhatkal, Distt. North Kanara 581 320, Karnal.
Sharfuddin and Sons, Booksellers, 29, M.A. Road, Bombay-400 003, Maharashtra.
Sheikh Mohd. Usman and Sons, Exchange Road, Yowkadal Chowk, Srinagar-190 001, J & K.
Sheikh Moslehuddin, Booksellers, 362, 2nd Block, Jayanagar, Bangalore-560 011, Karnataka.
Siddiq-e-Jadeed Book Agency, Kutchery Road, Lucknow, 226 001, U.P.
Star Publications, 66, Big Street, Triplicane, Madras-600 005, T.N.
Student's Book House, Charminar, Hyderabad-500 002, A.P.
Taj Office, Md. Ali Road, Bombay-400 003, Maharashtra.
Taj Publishing Co., 3151, Turkman Gate, Delhi-110 006.
Taleem ul Islam Book Depot, 642, Triplicane, Madras-600 005, T.N.
Urdu Library Centre, Booksellers, 11, 1st Floor, City Market, Bangalore-560 002, Karnataka.
Usmania Kutub Khana, Bhindi Bazar, Bombay-400 003, Maharashtra.
Urdu Book Depot, Outside Hathipole, Udaipur, 313 001, Rajasthan.
Yousuf Bros, Booksellers, Hathipole, Udaipur, 313 001, Rajasthan.
Zafar Book Deport, Kutcherry Road, Gaya, 823 001, Bihar.

Reputed Agencies

Allied Publishers, 13/14, Asaf Ali Road, New Delhi-110 002.
Alvi Book Depot, 49, M.A. Road, Bombay-400 003, Maharashtra.
Amar Prakashan, A1/139, B. Lawrence Road, Delhi-110 035.
Ambica Publications, 54, Tagore Gardens, New Delhi-110 001.
Asia Publishing House, Calicut Street, Bellard Estate, Bombay-400 001, Maharashtra.
Biblia Impex Pvt. Ltd. 2/18, Ansari Road, New Delhi-110 002.
Bihar Book Depot, Khazanchi Road, Patna-800 004, Bihar.
Book Traders, Kothi Bus Stand, Hyderabad-500 001, A.P.
Cambridge University Press, 139, Munirka Enclave, New Delhi-110 067.
Centre for Asian Documentation, P.B. 11215, Calcutta-700 014, West Bengal.
Concept Publishing Company, A/15-16, Commercial Block, Mohan Garden, New Delhi-110 059.
Crown, 225 Park Avenue, 5, New York-100 03, N.Y.
D.K. Publishers, 1 Ansari Road, New Delhi-110 002.
Gyan Publishing House, 29/6, Shakti Nagar, Delhi-110 007.
Graphic Aids, 19, Gulmohar Park, New Delhi-110 049.
A.A. Husain and Co., Abid Road, Hyderabad-500 001, A.P.
Informatics, 44, Gurukrupa, P.B. 2025, Seshadripuram, Bangalore-560 020, Karnataka.
Indian Bibliographies Bureau, Chah Indara, Fountain, Delhi-110 006.
Indian Documentation Service, P.B.13, Gurgaon-122 001, Haryana.
Kalinga Pub., 10A, Pocket I, Mayur Vihar, Delhi-110 001.
Kokil Book Depot, 49, M.A. Road, Bombay-400 003, Maharashtra.
Manohar Publications, 1 Ansari Road, Daryaganj, New Delhi-110 002.
Meenakshi Prakashan, Begum Bridge, Meerut-250 001, U.P.
Metropolitan Book Co., 1, Netaji Subhash Marg, Delhi-110 006.
Motilal Banarsidas, Bungalow Road, Jawahar Nagar, Delhi-110 007.
Munshiram Manoharlal, P.B. No. 5715, 54, Rani Jhansi Road, New Delhi-110 055.
Nai Naslen Pub. Shamshad Market, Aligarh-202 001, U.P.
New and Secondary Book Shop, 526, Kalbadevi Road, Bombay-400 002, Maharashtra.
New Order Book Co., Ellis Bridge, Ahmedabad-380 006, Gujarat.
Orient Longmans, 315, Asaf Ali Road, New Delhi-110 002.

Orient Book Co., C29/31, College Street, 1st Floor, Calcutta-700 007, W.B.

Oriental Book Agency, 15, Shukrawar Peth, Pune-411 002, Maharashtra.

Oriental Publishers, 1488, Pataudi House, Daryaganj, New Delhi-110 002.

Oriental Watchman Pub. House, Salishoury Park, P.B. No. 35, Pune-411 001, Maharashtra.

Oxford University Press, YMCA Library Building, P.B. No. 43, New Delhi-110 001.

Poona Oriental Book House, 1015, Sadashivpeth, Pune-411 002, Maharashtra.

Renaissance Publishing House, C-69, Jitar Nagar, Delhi-110 051.

R. Sheshadri, 32, Second Main Road, C.I.T. East, Madras-600 035, T. Nadu.

Seemant Prakashan, 922, Kucha Rohella Khan, New Delhi-110 002.

Sterling Pub., AB 9, Safdarjang Development Area, New Delhi-110 016.

D.B. Taraporevala, 210 D.N. Road, Bombay-400 001, Maharashtra.

Taraporevala Block-C, 13th Floor, 67, D.G. Marg, Bombay-400 026, Maharashtra.

N.M. Tripathi, 164, Samaldas Gandhi Marg, Bombay-400 003, Maharashtra.

Vikas Pub. House, 576, Masjid Road, New Delhi-110 014.

5. GLOSSARY OF INDIAN/ISLAMIC TERMS

GLOSSARY OF INDIAN/ISLAMIC TERMS

Adab (A)	Literature; Civility, rules; manners; etiquette; salutation (greetings)
Adat (A)	Habit; custom; practice
Adhan (A) (mis spelt *Azan*)	Calling for prayer
Alim (A)	*See* Maulana
Amanat (A)	See Maulana
Allama (A)	Trust
Anjuman (P)	Association; Society
Apa (T)	Elder sister
Aqida (A)	Faith; creed
Aqidat (A)	Belief in some one; great respect for saint; etc.
Aqiqa (A)	Seventhday child birth rite
Aqlaq (A)	Ethics; manners
Ashraf (A) (Pl. of Sharif)	Noble
As *salam lai kum* (A)	Greeting; a prayer for peace
Auliya (A)	*See* Waliyyullah
Aurat (A)	Women
Awam (A)	Public
Azan	*See* Adhan
Bada (H)	Big; large; old
Badshah (P)	King (ruler)
Bait (A)	Allegiance (mystical); distich (poetical); house
Bait at Mal (A)	Treasury
Baji (T)	Big sister

---

* A = Arabic; H = Hindi; P = Persian; S = Sanskrit T = Turkish

Bakr'Id (H) (*Idul Adha*)	Festival of sacrifice
Banda (P)	Slave
Baras (H)	Year
Barai (H)	Superiority; greatness
Barsat (H)	Rains
Batin (A)	Esoteric
Bawarchi	Cook
Bazar (P)	Market
Begum (T)	Wife; noble-women
Behen (H)	Sister
Beta (H)	Son; boy
Beti (H)	Daughter; girl
Bhayya (H)	Brother; elder brother
Biryani (P)	Rice and meet cooked together with spices
Bismillah (A)	To commence in the name of *Allah*; opening ceremony
Burai (H)	Evil; mischief
Burhapa (H)	Old age
Burqa (A)	*See purdah*
Chisti (P)	Follower of *Chishti silsila*
Chota (H)	Small
Dada (H)	Paternal grand-father
Dadi (H)	Paternal grand-mother
Dalil (A)	Reason; proof
Dar ul-Harb (A)	Non-Muslim country
Dar al-Islam (A)	Muslim country
Dar as shifa (A)	Hospital
Darogha (A)	Inspector; manager
Darud (A)	Invoke God's blessings on the Holy Prophet
Darul Mutalia (A)	*See Kutub Khana*
Darul Qaza (A)	Court of Law
Darul Uloom (A)	Centre of learning; see also *Madrasa; Jamia*
Darvesh (P)	Mendicant; *see* also Faqir
Darwaza (P)	Entryway
Dawa (A)	Invitation; call (used for propagation)
Diwan-e-Khas (P)	Privy Council
Diwan-i-Aam (P)	Public hall of audience
Divan (P)	Prime Ministers Secretariat

Doha (H)	Hindi Couplet; *see* also *Bait*
Dua (A)	Supplication; Prayer
Faiz (A)	Grace
Faqir (A)	Beggar; *darvesh*
Faqr (A)	Obligatory
Farz (A)	*See Faqir*
Fasiq/Fajir (A)	Adulterator; Sinner
Fasli (A)	Persian solar calendar; Revenue Year; Harvest season
Fatiha (A)	Supplication; prayer
Fatwa (A)	Religious ruling
Fiqh (A)	Islamic jurisprudence
Ghodswari (H)	Horsemanship
Ghair Soodi (P)	Interest free
Hadith (A)	Documented traditions of the Prophet
Hadya (A)	Gift; cost of a religious book
Hakim (P)	Unani doctor
Halwai (A&H)	Sweet-meet seller.
Haram (A)	Women's apartment; sacred area of Mecca
Haveli (A)	Palace; Palatial residence
Hazir (A)	Present
Hazrat (A)	Sir
Hiba (A)	Gift
Hijab (A)	*See Purdah*
Hijri; Hijrah (A)	Muslim lunar calendar
Idul Adha (A)	*See Bakrid*
Ijab-va-qubul (A)	Proposal and consent in marriage negotiation
Ijma (A)	Consensus
Ijtihad (A)	Authoritative interpretation; independent reasoning
Ilm (A)	Knowledge
Iqtisadiyat (A)	Economics
Irshad (A)	Command
Islamiyat (A)	Islamic studies; Islamics
Ism nawisi (A&P)	List of witnesses
Isnad (A)	Chain of *Hadith* narrators
Istihsan (A)	Decision based on relative considerations
Istikhara (A)	Judging from dreams

Istislah (A)	Decision for public good
Istisqa (A)	Prayer for rain
Itiqad (A)	*See Aqida*
Jagir (P)	Land granted
Jahil (A)	Permitted
Jaiz (A)	Ignorant
Jamia (A)	University; *Madrasa*
Jan (P)	Dear
Janaza (A)	Bier
Jawaz (A)	Permission
Jihad (A)	Striving righteously
Kabutar (P)	Pigeon; dove
Katib (A)	Scribe (literary); secretary (archaic)
Khala (A)	Maternal aunt
Khalu (A)	Maternal aunt's husband
Khanqah (A)	Hospiece; convent
Khatib (A)	Sermonizer
Khatna (A)	Circumcision
Khula (A)	Divorce obtained on wife's initiative
Khutba (A)	Sermon
Khwaja (P)	Lord; Master
Kichdi (H)	A preparation of rice and dal together
Kos (H)	Approximately more than three kilometres
Kufr (A)	Impiety; irreligion; infidelity
Kuniyyat (A)	Family name; patronymic appellation
Kutubkhana (A&P)	Library
Lachar (H)	*See nachar*
Maashiyat (A)	Economy
Madariya	A follower of Shah Madar
Madrasa (A)	College
Mahr (A)	A gift settled for the wife; alimony; Dower; jointure
Majlis (A)	Assembly
Makruh (A)	Prohibited; abominable
Maktab (A)	Primary school; *Quranic* school
Maktaba (A)	Bookshop; (rare) library
Mamu (H)	Paternal uncle
Mannat (H)	Promise; vow
Mardana (P)	Drawing room for men

Masail (A)	Percepts of the Prophet Muhammad
Maslahat (H)	Legal proposition; fitness
Maslak (A)	Law School
Maulana (A)	Muslim scholar, *see* also *Maulvi*
Maulud (A)	Prophet's birthday celebration
Maulvi (A)	Teacher; learned person, *see* also *Maulana*
Meraj (A)	Holy Prophet's ascension to Heaven
Mihrab (A)	Niche in the Mosque
Mimbar (A)	Pulpit in the Mosque
Miras (A)	Inheritance
Mirza (P)	Prince
Mizaj (A)	Condition of health
Muallim (A)	*See Maulvi*
Mubah (A)	Optional
Mubarak (A)	Greetings
Mudarat (A)	Courtesy
Mufti (A)	Juriconsult; one who gives *fatwa*
Muhalla (A)	Locality; area; a quarter or part of a town
Mujaddid (A)	Reformer
Mujahid (A)	One who participates in *jihad*
Mujizah (A)	Miracle
Mujtahid (A)	Any learned scholar who takes independent decisions
Mulla (A)	*See Maulana*
Munazira (A)	Disputation
Murid (A)	Novice; mystic disciple
Murraghan (P)	Oily
Murshed (A)	*See Pir*
Musalla (A)	Prayer carpet
Musalmani	*See Khatna*
Mustahab (A)	Praiseworthy
Mutawalli (A)	Trustee
Nachari (P&H)	Helpless
Nafil (A)	Supererogatory prayers
Nana (H)	Maternal grand-father
Nani (H)	Maternal grand-mother
Naqshbandi	A follower of *Naqshbandi silsila*
Naskh (A)	A caligraphic style; Arabic script
Nastaaliq (P)	Urdu and Persian caligraphic style

Nawab (A)	Noble prince
Nawasa (P)	Grand-child; son; daughter
Nawasi (P)	Grand-child; daughter's daughter
Nikah (A)	Marriage performed according to Islamic Law
Nikhattu (H)	Useless person
Niyat (A)	Intension
Ojhal (H)	Concealed; invisible
Padri (P)	Clergyman
Pagri (H)	Goodwill
Pak (P)	Clean; pure
Palao (also pulau) (P)	*See Biryani*
Pan (H)	Betal leaf
Pani (H)	Water
Para (H)	Mercury
Parsa (P)	Chaste; virtuous; holy
Pas (H)	Nearby
Pasban (P&H)	Guard; sentinel
Pathar (H)	Hard
Phupha (H)	Paternal aunt's husband
Phuphi (H)	Paternal aunt
Pir (P)	Spiritual guide
Pota (H)	Grandchild; son of a son
Poti (H)	Grandchild; daughter of a son
Pulau	*See Palao*
Punkha (H)	Fan
Puri (H)	Bread
Pyjama (P)	Loose pant
Qadri	A follower of *Qadri silsila*
Quida (A)	Guide; primer
Qanun (A)	Law
Qari (A)	Recitor of *Quran*
Qasam (A)	Oath
Qazi (A)	Judge
Qibla (A)	Director of prayer; venerable person
Qirat (A)	Musical recitation of *Quran*
Qisas (A)	Retaliation
Qiyas (A)	Reasoning by analogy
Qurbani (A)	Sacrifice in the name of *Allah*

Rae (A)	Opinion of the Ulama
Riba (A)	Interest
Ribat (correct form of) *Rubat)* (A)	Camp; monastary
Roti (H)	Bread
Sadaqa (A)	Charitable offering
Sahabi (A)	A companion of the Prophet Muhammad
Sahib (A)	Sir
Sahebzada (P)	Son of a nobleman
Sair (A)	Tour
Sajjada nashin (P)	Shrine superior
Salam (A)	*See Assalamu lai-kum*
Sala (H)	Wife's brother
Salar (P)	Leader
Salar-e-Jang (P)	Commander-in-Chief
Samaajiyat (H)	Social studies; sociology
Samna (H)	Facing; confronting
Samne (H)	Before; opposite; in front
Samraj (S)	Imperialism
Sanad (A)	Degree; contract; proof
Sanp (P)	Snake
Sayyid (A)	Lord; Nobleman;
Serai (P)	Travellers' Bunglow
Shab-e-Barat (A)	14th Night of the Muslim calendar month Shaban
Shahid (A)	Martyr; witness
Shaikh (A)	Elder; Chieftan
Sharia (A)	Islamic Law
Sharif	*See Ashraf*
Shia (A)	Followers of Ali
Shirk (A)	Polytheism; Idolatory; infidality
Silsila (A)	Chain (mystical)
Sirat (A)	Biography of Prophets and Saints
Sufi (A)	Mystic
Suharwardi	Follower of *Suherrwardi Silsila*
Sunni (A)	Orthodox Muslim
Tabedar (P)	Servant; follower
Tabligh (A)	*See Dawa*
Tahjjud (A)	A prayer said after mid-night

Talaq (A)	Divorce
Talim (A)	Teaching
Taqlid (A)	Following a legal decision based on past authority
Taqiya (A)	Permissible subterfuge; fear
Tarawi (A)	Night prayers of Ramadhan
Tarikh (A)	History; date
Tariqa (A)	Way (mystical)
Tasawwuf (A)	Sufism
Tashih (A)	Correction; verification
Tashrif (A)	Honouring; exalting
Taslim (A)	Greeting
Tawaf (A)	Circumambulation of Kaba
Tawassal (A)	Mediation
Tawhid (A)	Oneness of God
Tawil (A)	Allegorical interpretation
Tayyamum (A)	Ablution of clean earth
Taziya (A)	Condolence
Tazir (A)	Curative punishment
Topi (H)	Cap
Tu (H)	You
Tum (H)	You
Ulama (Pl. of Alim) (A)	*See Maulana*
Ummah (A)	Muslim Community
Umraniyat (A)	*See Samaajiyat*
Ustad (A)	Teacher
Usul (A)	Fundamental rules
Vatan (A)	Native
Virasat (A)	Inheritance; legacy
Wahhabi (A)	Staunch Muslim; follower of Abdul Wahhab
Wajib (A)	Essential
Wakf (A)	Endowment for public utility
Wali (A)	Guardian; *see* also *Waliyyullah*
Waliyyullah (A)	Saint
Waris (A)	Inheritor
Wasiya (A)	Will
Wilayat (A)	Office of a saint
Witr (A)	Night Prayers in odd numbers

Wuzu (A)	Ablution
Yaqin (A)	Certitude
Zahed (A)	Abstinent; Hermit
Zahir (A)	Exteric
Zakat (A)	Enjoined charity
Zanana (P)	Women's quarters
Zuban (P)	Language; tongue
Zikr (A)	Remembrances of Allah
Zina (A)	Formication
Zindiq (A)	Heretic

6. SOURCES CONSULTED

SOURCES CONSULTED

Ahmed, Syed Barakat "Myth of Resurgence", *Seminar* No. 290, (1983), 14-15.

All India Book Trade Directory. Delhi, Modern Publications, 1979.

BEPI: Bibliography of English Publications in India, Delhi D.K.F. Trust, 1979.

Books in Print, 1988-89, New York, Bowker, 1988, 7 Vols.

Calcutta Telephone Directory, 1988.

Commonwealth Universities Handbook, 1988, 4 V.

Comprehensive Dissertation Index, 1973–1977. Ann Arbor, U.M.I., 1979.

Dandekar R.N. and V. Raghavan, *Oriental Studies in India*, 1964.

Delhi Telephone Directory, 1988.

Desai, Ziauddin, *Centres of Islamic Learning in India*, New Delhi, Min. of I and B, 1978.

Directory of Delhi Authors, New Delhi, Authors Guild of India, 1982.

Dissertation Abstracts International, Ann Arbor, U.M.I.

Gidwani, N.N. and K. Navalani, *Guide to Reference Materials on India*, Jaipur, Saraswati Pub., 1974, 2V.

Growther, G., *et al.*, *India a Travel Survival Kit*. Victoria, Lonely Plant Pub., 1984.

Holmes, H.W., Research Facilities Series (See list of *Reference Sources*).

Hyderabad Telephone Directory, 1989.

India Who's Who, 1988-89, 19th ed. New Delhi, INFA, 1989.

Indian Books in Print, 1988, New Delhi, Indian Bibliographies Bureau, 1988, 3V.

Inter-University Board of India, New Delhi. *Bibliography of Doctoral Dissertations, Accepted by Indian Universities, 1857-1970*, 1975, V.3 and V.5.

JNU Dissertations Index, New Delhi, 198

Jain N.K., *Muslims in India: A Biographical Dictionary*, New Delhi Manohar, 1979-1983, 2V.

Khan, M.A.S., *Directory of Islamic Libraries and Librarians* (*a sample of the World*), California, Islamic Lib. Association, 1983.

Madras Telephone Directory, 1989

MAP's Road Atlas of India, Madras, Tamilnad Printers and Traders, 1982

Moghni, Abdul "World of Islam", *Islamic Service: A Magazine of Thought and Opinion* (1984)

Nadvi, S. Abul Hasan, *Islamic Studies, Orientalists and Muslim Scholars*, Lucknow, Academy of Islamic Research and Publications, 1983.

National Register of Doctoral Dissertations Accepted and in Progress in Social Sciences and Humanities in Indian Universities, Bhopal, Council of Oriental Res., 1980. 2 pts.

"Oriental Libraries in India: A Directory", *ILA Bulletin* 17 (1981) 153-69.

Panwar, B.S. and S.D. Vyas, *Directory of Libraries, Publishers, and Booksellers of Udaipur City and Who's Who*, Guregaon, Prabhu Book Service, 1970.

Ranjan, B., *South Indian Studies: Abstracts of American Doctoral Dissertations relating to India*, Salem, Inst. of Kongu Studies, 1981.

Said Edward, *Orientalism*, London, Routledge, 1978.

Satyaprakash, *Muslims in India: A Bibliography of their religious, socio-economic and political literature*. Gurgaon, Indian Documentation Service, 1985.

Siddiqui, Mohd. Himayutul Muqeet, *Alam-e-Islam Padhrveen Sadhi ke Darwaze per*, Rampur, Maktaba Zikra, 1981.

Singh, Mohinder, *Learned Societies and Institutions in India: Activities and Publications*, Delhi, Metropolitan Book Co., 1975.

Siraj, Maqbool Ahmed, "Electoral Demography of Indian Muslims", *J. Inst. Minority Affairs* 7 (1980), 557-603.

Southern R.W., *Western Views of Islam in the Middle Ages* Cambridge, Harvard U. Pr. 1978.

Study Abroad: International Scholarships and International Courses, Paris, UNESCO, 1983.

Taher, Mohamed and Abdul Majeed Pangal, Bibliographical Control of Islamic Literature in India: "Perspectives", *Islamic Culture*, 58 (1984), 161-169.

Taher Mohamed, Mohammed Burhanuddin and A.A. Khan, Madrasa Libraries in India, *International Library Review*, 1989, (contains description, analysis of seven Madrasas in six cities). Dargah Libraries in India *International Library Review*, 1986 (contains Descriptive analysis of five Dargahs in four cities).

Times of India Year Book, 1982.

"Theses of the Month" in *University News*, New Delhi

Tyagi, K.G., *Foreign Researches on Indian Political Systems and Processes*, Delhi, Pinka Agencies, 1984.

Ulrich's International Periodicals Directory, 1987-88

Usmani S.A. and Z.R. Khan "Oriental Libraries in India", in *Perspectives in Library and Information Science*, Lucknow, Print House, 1982, pp

Watt, M.M. "Islam and Tomorrow's World", *Islamic Culture* 59 (1985) 261.

Who's Who of Indian Writers, 1983, New Delhi, Sahitya Akademy, 1983.

World of Learning, 1987 Europa.

Writers Directory, 1984-86, London, Macmillan, 1983.

Yasufuddin, M., *Oriental and Islamic Studies in World Universities*, Hyderabad, Islamic Publications Society, 1953.